Nature-Inspired Learning and Leading

REVEALING AND APPLYING
NATURE'S WISDOM

Stephen B. Jones

Scripture taken from the King James Version of the Bible.

LifeRich Publishing is a registered trademark of The Reader's Digest Association, Inc.

LifeRich Publishing books may be ordered through booksellers or by contacting:

LifeRich Publishing
1663 Liberty Drive
Bloomington, IN 47403
www.liferichpublishing.com
1 (888) 238-8637

ISBN: 978-1-4897-1309-4 (sc)
ISBN: 978-1-4897-1310-0 (hc)
ISBN: 978-1-4897-1308-7 (e)

Library of Congress Control Number: 2017909496

Print information available on the last page.

LifeRich Publishing rev. date: 06/26/2017

Contents

Dedication

I dedicate this book to four people who have touched me deeply and served as role models and mentors.

Dr. Glenn O. Workman, professor emeritus at Allegany College of Maryland (ACM), recruited me into the brand new, two-year, pre-professional Forestry Program at ACM, which at the time (1969) was Allegany Community College, in Cumberland, Maryland. Doc inspired me, believed in me, and ushered me from high school through ACC to one of the nation's top five forestry programs at SUNY Environmental Science and Forestry at Syracuse. We have stayed close over the more than four decades since then. Two years ago, Judy and I established an ACM scholarship in Doc's name as a small token of our deep appreciation.

Dr. Robert C. Kellison, professor emeritus at NC State University, stands among those who have marked me indelibly. I have known Bob since my Union Camp days. (I left the company in 1985). Like Doc, Bob believed in me and may have had some small influence on my sense of humor! We both take what we do seriously; yet take ourselves less so.

Dr. Cary Keller, who authored one of this book's guest essays, is a dear friend who has selflessly supported and championed me beginning with my term as University of Alaska Fairbanks Chancellor. As team physician, he sewed seven stitches on my right hand during the first period of a Nanook D-I hockey match: a game injury I suffered (by falling while racing up to my seat). You'll see in these essays that Cary accompanied me on three all-night charity bicycle rides in Ohio. He is one of my heroes.

Dr. Ernie Muller, deceased Syracuse University geomorphology professor emeritus, stands as the best instructor of my long collegiate studies. I took his course during my doctoral program. He planted the seed for the descriptive, passion-fueled writing about nature that I do. That germinant, now growing beyond the sapling stage, is flourishing today; in his honor I tend and nurture the tree daily. He worked closely with me challenging, guiding, and coaching my writing. I will always remember the supreme satisfaction I drew from occasionally getting it right. He lifted me to a new level, and for that I shall always be grateful.

To these four wonderful gentlemen, I dedicate *Nature-Inspired Learning and Leading*.

Acknowledgments

Judy has inspired my entire adult life: four years of dating and 45 years married. Nothing beats sharing life and dreams with a best friend. She encouraged *Nature Based Leadership*, my first book; she lifted me through this second book. As I said in the acknowledgments to the first book, she is the wind beneath my wings. There is nobody else with whom I'd rather share a sunrise … or a sunset. She is my courage.

I also acknowledge and thank Cary Gaunt for writing the foreword, and my dear friends and colleagues for their accompanying reflective essays: Bob Benton, Ray Silverman, Cary Keller, Jeff Patnaude, and Jennifer Wilhoit. Jennifer also performed superbly as editor—what a pleasure!

I offer a special thank you to Jim McGill, former Johns Hopkins University Senior Vice President for Finance and Administration, for contributing $2,500 to support editing. Jim and I are kindred souls; I am grateful for his contribution and for his belief in me. Jim donated his gift through the Alabama A&M University Forestry, Ecology, and Wildlife Program where I serve as adjunct faculty. Dr. WES Stone serves as Program Coordinator. I am grateful to be affiliated with such an exemplary forestry education unit.

I also want to thank Matt Jones, our son, and Katy Disher, our daughter, for their love and the five grandchildren in aggregate they have brought into our lives: Hannah, Mallory, and Nathan (Matt's), and Jack and Sam (Katy's).

Because of the people who have believed in me, and owing to nature's beauty, awe, magic, and wonder, life is good! May all of us recognize and act upon our obligation to steward this one earth.

Foreword

Those of us engaged in environmental and sustainability work struggle to identify the best ways to protect and restore ecological and social systems. Our nation's historic efforts have yielded significant progress. Yet, time and time again we fall short of our goals, or our incremental progress is agonizingly slow. Too often a success story is met by a new challenge.

We evaluate our approaches, try new ones, fully embrace the tenets of adaptive management; yet critical environmental and social thresholds are increasingly met and exceeded. Patterns of water quality degradation, global climate change, natural land and biodiversity loss, species extinction, and social injustice are alarming.

There is something deeper going on, something at the core of what it means to be human and how we are called to live. It is something that we cannot study, educate, monitor, model, regulate, negotiate, or fix with new technologies, although these are essential pieces of a very complex puzzle. The International Earth Charter calls for a "new beginning … [that] requires a change of mind and heart," and Pope Francis describes the need for an "integral ecology … which transcend[s] the language of mathematics and biology, and take[s] us to the heart of what it is to be human" (Encyclical 2015). There is a chorus of similar calls from around the world.

Dr. Steve Jones explores these issues head on in this collection of essays. Reflecting on his 44 years as a "lifetime champion of nature," lover of natural sciences, and forestry-trained semi-retired university/college president, Steve describes his personal journey of stepping out of the "zone of comfort" as a higher education leader and into the "zone of courage" as scholar, author, speaker, and consultant to bring his concept of Nature Based Leadership to the world. The root of the word courage is *coeur*, meaning "heart." And Steve's book resonates with heart as he describes in vivid stories how Nature Based Leadership presents "a new way of looking, seeing, feeling, and acting." Steve articulates his personal journey—how the early seeds of Nature Based Leadership were planted and nourished, to the present moment where he boldly and bravely steps forward to apply his wisdom, training, and passion to "preaching the gospel of responsible Earth stewardship."

I was fortunate to meet Steve over harvest dinner at a lovely country setting in southern New Hampshire in September 2013. My own inquiry into the root causes of environmental decline circuitously led me to this moment as an alumna of Antioch University New England's Doctoral Program in Environmental Studies, where Steve had just started as president. My road to AUNE some 13 years prior began after more than 16 years leading watershed management efforts around the country, but primarily with the Chesapeake Bay, my home watershed. The trajectory of my personal and professional life was dramatically changed at the turn of the millennia by an unusual siren's call in the form of the capstone conclusion from a visionary report by long-term colleagues and clients of the Chesapeake Bay Program partnership.

In 2003 the Chesapeake Bay Program, long recognized as the standard-bearer for watershed and environmental restoration, released *Chesapeake Futures: Choices for the 21st Century,* a comprehensive retrospective of its 20-year restoration approach. Over 30 scientists and managers concluded that despite progress in science and technology, "the kind of Bay our children inherit will depend on the choices we make at the dawn of this new century...at the heart of everything is what we shall call a change of consciousness" (Boesch & Greer, Eds., pp. 7 & 20). What's needed is "cultivating a new ethic: the enlightened citizen."

The question is, how? How do we cultivate the [ecologically] enlightened citizen and leader? This is the question I picked up for my doctoral research at AUNE, and the one I continue with in my new academic and vocational focus on holistic sustainability. I blend teaching with practice as the Director of Campus Sustainability at Keene State College, a role in which I am always seeking effective methods for integrating the outer, inner, and leadership dimensions of sustainability. It is also the question that engaged Steve and me in conversation after dinner back in 2013.

To change the trajectory of our global environmental and social justice challenges, we need people from all sectors to enthusiastically embrace these clarion calls for a change in consciousness, an ecological enlightenment from their unique vantage points. This is the important contribution Steve Jones offers in this book and through the founding of a NBLI at AUNE when he was president there. Nature Based Leadership provides one pathway toward cultivating ecological enlightenment: the essential transformation of hearts, minds, and action.

Returning to that September dinner when I first met Steve, I recall our meander around the gardens and meadow of our host's home. Steve commented on the geology, bird song, trees, flowers, and vegetables, noticing and inquiring with the keen eyes of a naturalist and the mind of a geographer. But his joy, enthusiasm, curiosity, and appreciation (dare I say "love") for the creatures and the creation were palpable: far beyond a mere intellectual exercise. Steve was demonstrating Nature Based Leadership in action. It was clear he had embodied the intention he fully claims in this book, "to devote [his] professional years…to Earth stewardship."

We need leaders who will do that. Fundamental to a new way of doing business is seeing ourselves as *part of* the natural world and the places we inhabit, instead of *apart from*. Perhaps the taproot of a sustainability ethic is kinship—something our indigenous forebears, historical environmental heroes, and today's sustainability role models embody—a deep sense of belonging, where humans are embedded in their places and connected to the natural world in relational and participatory ways. This is a more indigenous way of knowing, described by Native American educator and Tewa Indian Gregory

Cajete, as one that is rooted in place and based on "the perception gained from using the entire body of our senses in direct participation with the natural world." This perceptual wisdom is far broader than the narrow view of western science and business management because dynamic participation with the natural world opens us to spirituality, a broader sense of community, richer understanding of interdependence and reciprocity, and qualities of wonder and gratitude that are essential for sustainability. And this is what Steve believes, lives, and seeks to bring forth with Nature Based Leadership. He writes, "I find inspiration, solace, and illumination in the natural world. I have believed for some time that the lessons of leadership and life are written in nature more indelibly, powerfully, and succinctly than any management text could possibly encapsulate."

Later that same evening, over post-dinner beverages, we conversed more about Steve's foundational beliefs for Nature Based Leadership, especially his conviction that "Nature-Inspired Learning and Leading encompasses far more than cold, empirical, objective consideration of fact and context." That engaging the "five human portals" is essential and "spirit is paramount in living, learning, serving, and leading." Here we found a strong resonance as my journey into the inquiry of how to cultivate the ecologically enlightened person led me to a similar destination, albeit through a very different path.

I sought out the wisdom of lived experience from individuals who are ecologically awakened and committed to sustainability—leaders and ordinary citizens who modeled the kinds of changes we seek. Like Steve, these exemplars experienced a necessary alignment of their minds *and* hearts that led to outward action. They were deeply informed about science, but did not stop there; deep commitments to faith and spiritual practice provided the fertile ground for their lives to speak. In their work and lives, as Steve proposes with Nature Based Leadership, their commitment to environmental stewardship was deepened by a more holistic approach, one that integrates into the existing science and technology the other side of the human coin: values and priorities such as spirituality, beauty, and wonder.

"I find no better roots for NBL than in a substrate that is deeply spiritual (or, in this case, Spiritual). I wrote in *Nature Based Leadership* of the absolute humility and inspiration I felt the first time I viewed Denali, North America's tallest peak, up close from nearby Mt. Quigley. Seldom do I witness and experience the wonder of Nature without spiritual movement, spurring deep feelings in mind, heart, and soul. I cannot think of NBL without engaging Spirit."

A perceived setback (described in the preface and Chapter 1 of this book) brought Steve to his current vocation. Quoting Bernard Malamud, Steve understands, "We have two lives to live; the life we learn with and the life we live after that" (1952, p. 237). Steve is currently embracing his "second" life, spawned by his deep reflection and introspection that courageously occurred during challenging times.

This book is a testimony to the wisdom that emerged from that inward look. Above all, Steve is an exquisite storyteller, and through his personal anecdotes and rich descriptions of the natural world, he describes his personal evolution from the comfort of paid institutional work to his vocation of Nature Based Leadership in its emerging forms. As a person who studies the life journeys of leaders and role models, I found this collection of essays fascinating. Steve provides glimpses of his early formative experiences and how those informed his nascent concept of Nature Based Leadership and the maturing vision of NBLI and now Great Blue Heron, LLC. My initial dinner conversation with Steve led to many future discussions and the privilege to work beside him in the early stages of the Nature Based Leadership Institute he founded at AUNE. Both of us have gone onto other venues, yet the core tenets of Nature Based Leadership inform the work each of us does.

This book of essays shares the evolution of a person, leader, and important concept for our times: Nature Based Leadership. Steve's call is clear: to offer his "passion-fueled desire to give life and vibrancy to the emerging discipline of Nature Based Leadership" so that "leaders, present and future, understand and embrace the concept and practice of nature-based and nature-inspired leadership." This book, the second in a trilogy of works Steve is preparing, provides rich reading and inspiration for those seeking new sources of wisdom for 21st century leadership and living.

Cary H. Gaunt, Ph.D.
Director of Sustainability
Keene State College

Preface

Forty-four years beyond earning a BS in forestry, I have come to believe that every lesson for living, learning, serving, and leading is either written indelibly *in*, or is compellingly inspired *by* nature. Over the past three years, colleagues (old and new) have encouraged me to further develop the concept and memorialize its precepts and tenets. To that end, several of us launched a still-emerging Nature Based Leadership Institute (NBLI) in 2015, housed at Antioch University New England (AUNE), where I served as president through June 30, 2016.

I had gone to AUNE intending for that presidency to be my swan song, leading to retirement sometime after 2021. Antioch University New England is one of the five campuses of Antioch University. However, the Antioch University Governing Board eliminated the five campus presidents, their administrative assistants, and the campus boards of trustees effective immediately (end of June 2016). As the NBLI creator, I retain my status as a NBLI founder, but without the responsibility of leading AUNE. I took advantage of my transition to president and CEO of Great Blue Heron, LLC: Nature-Inspired Learning and Leading, and completed my first book manuscript, handing it off to my editor, getting it to my publisher, and then shifting gears to address this second book. LifeRich published "Nature Based Leadership" in December 2016.

I have been developing the two sets of essays for years. You will see several in this second book that date back to summer 2011, and three from April 2010, 2011, and 2012. Interestingly, because my understanding, interpretation, and practice of my trade (leadership) is still emerging, evolving, and maturing, I have only recently reached a stage where I can bring real value to these nature-inspired lessons for living, learning, serving, and leading. It's not so much that these essays languished for years. Instead, they lay dormant, protected from what would have been my premature efforts to complete them. Like a seed germinating only after the danger of late frosts and freezes, these essays can now flourish in favorable conditions on fertile soil. As I consider all that comes next for me professionally, I can afford the time to tend the garden of thoughts, words, purpose, and passion. I am luxuriating in the unconstrained bounds of this unanticipated professional segue to full time engagement as scholar, author, speaker, and consultant.

I wrote the first book preface from southwestern New Hampshire. You may detect a southern drawl in this preface, written here in northern Alabama. Fortuitously, I had anticipated an impending Antioch University restructuring and placed our New Hampshire home for sale in early May 2016. We entertained an offer on the third day and reached sales price accord at two weeks. To evidence the role of a higher hand, we had completed our eventual retirement home near our daughter (and two grandsons) in northern Alabama the prior December. The moving crew packed and loaded our NH home contents on July 18 (my 65th birthday), and delivered the load in Huntsville on July 24. We closed on the NH sale July 22. Who says that life is not good, that divine providence is not at work?

I write these words as a former university/college president, a lifetime champion of nature, a natural resources scientist, and a leadership practitioner, scholar, author, and consultant. Writing the first book preface proved daunting; I'm finding this one no less difficult! I'm fighting the temptation to repeat the fundamental elements I addressed in the first. Not really fighting the temptation, I'm standing resolute, refusing to burden the second book reader with repeat verbiage. I must admit that I did consider repeating my definition of nature based leadership from that collection. I resisted. Not because I no longer subscribe to those words. Instead, I have moved beyond the comfort of residing within the nature based leadership construct, which I embraced and helped refine at AUNE during my tenure as president.

Nature's routes, processes, options, and outcomes seem infinite. In many ways they are; yet the desired outcome—species by species—is to succeed, reproduce, and sustain. The same holds true within our own enterprises. We seek to sustain. We make decisions based upon selected metrics of sustainability, be they economic, social, or environmental, or some combination thereof. I've learned (and nature has practiced the same forever) that there is seldom only one track or alternative for success. While there may be only one best solution, I have seldom seen the success options so narrowly constrained to a single one that is clearly optimal. Nature provides for contingency. I draw a parallel in assembling this book. The only concrete restriction I imposed was to not use an essay that is in the first book. That said, I have drafted additional essays beyond the scope of what can comprise this second book.

First, I narrowed the selection of essays for this collection to fifteen. My selection criteria included: degree of completion; my satisfaction with the message, lessons, style, and memories evoked; fit within the book's theme. My next major task was to order the essays in some preferred sequence. Clearly there is no optimum order, nor the one gold standard ordering methodology. I ultimately arranged them according to what felt right, and whether I could weave a thread connecting each one to the next.

I am satisfied, yet I feel certain that were I to place them aside for twelve to eighteen months, I would likely choose differently. But not necessarily better. There is no single best package, beyond that which at the time feels right to me. I am the one who must live with the choice, and navigate the course ahead. What if my editor rebels? Okay, then I stand ready to listen, evaluate, weigh the evidence and arguments presented, and make a decision. Robert Frost (*The Road Not Taken*) observed beautifully that life does not distill to perfect decisions:

"Two roads diverged in a wood, and I – I took the one less traveled by, And that has made all the difference."

This book begins by exploring a tough decision. Do I dare enter a new domain professionally? I wrestled with comfort and courage, two human attributes and attitudes that guide and direct our living, learning, serving, and leading. Faced with the dilemma (or was it blessing) of having my presidency eliminated at the tender age of sixty-five years, what do I do? What can I do? What should I do? Do I accept retirement, seek another presidency, or get serious about starting a new business? Decisions of that magnitude are not exclusive to any one stage of life and career, nor are they the sole domain of individuals. Any enterprise must deal with inflection-level choices: ones that challenge us to decide between comfort and courage. I chose courage, but not without agonizing introspection, which I describe in the first essay.

I chose to create Great Blue Heron, LLC (GBH), my consulting firm rooted in the tenets of nature-inspired learning and leading. My GBH tag line is pretty simple: "nature-inspired learning and leading; applying nature's wisdom to life and work." The second essay describes GBH's initial client projects, both fully aligned with nature-inspired learning and leading, and delves into my personal motivation to pay forward the faith, confidence, and wisdom that nature-inspired mentors have invested in me.

The third essay shifts to my April 2016 visit to the Wisdom Center for Inner Excellence in Virginia's northern Blue Ridge foothills, less than an hour from our nation's capital. The Center immerses leaders and prospective leaders in an onsite, inner journey of leadership discovery. The setting provides endless opportunity to enmesh participants in nature based leadership; to lure them through intimate, mountaintop contact to see their place in the larger world; and to learn from nature's ways. As a forester, natural resources scientist, and practitioner of nature based leadership, I developed this essay as a philosophical musing. I am convinced that the tenets, principles, and imperatives inspired by nature can be practiced, taught, and demonstrated in many natural environments, not exclusively there on Viewtree Mountain.

Not long after that Blue Ridge foothill exercise, the Center's founder alerted me to a quote from a subsequent Sunday's church service: "The leaves of the tree are for the healing of the nations." He knew my forestry training (and nature-inspired passion) would lead me to reflect and respond. He knows me well; and the fourth essay is the result. Contemplating the quote led me to conclude that the entire earth is our tree of life. Nature-inspired learning and leading reminds us that we must tend our one earth, for it is our source of life.

The fifth essay herein is an edited transcript of the video presentation I prepared for an April 2015 presentation to a risk mitigation and value creation conference in San Francisco. I hope it evidences the tremendous formative thinking and distillation I invested in that earlier foray into defining and explaining nature-inspired learning and leading.

I find nature's inspiration from many sources. The May 2016 Antioch University New England student commencement speaker, Dr. Jason Rhodes, inspired the next essay. He spoke of success emerging over time, suggesting that—although the moment of fruition and accomplishment seems sudden—the effort expended on day one contributes as much to the outcome as the final push, the finishing. He mentioned the San Andreas Fault as an example from nature of how inexorable small actions over time can lead to momentous results. I carried his postulate a bit further in my essay here.

Next, I introduce the notion that so much in nature—as in life and vocation—lies concealed to all but the most knowing and discerning. Here you will read about "opening our eyes to the unseen in nature and in life," the essay's tagline.

Three fundraising bike rides to fight cancer generated palpable lessons from nature during my tenure as Urbana University president. Over consecutive Relay for Life events, I rode to raise money via pledges per mile. I've included three essays in sequence to present nature based lessons inspired by those nights on the trail.

From long nights of sometimes-wild weather and full exposure, one of the last essays shifts to nature's benign side, and a less frenetic pace. During my several years in southwestern New Hampshire, I discovered, adopted, and nurtured a frog pond on my four-acre domain. I learned a great deal about myself as I labored and observed.

I reached back five years for the next three essays: short reflections built around memories I captured in writing late summer and fall 2011, predating emergence of my explicit nature-inspired learning and leading musings. The papers document discrete experiences during a summer vacation to the Pacific Northwest. I draw lessons from a powerful, diurnal tidal flush at Nisqually National Wildlife Refuge; a journey of perspective crossing the Strait of Juan de Fuca; contemplating nature's extremes on Hurricane Ridge.

I complete this second book by bringing my dad back into the story. He's been gone 21 years, yet he remains with me: in spirit, soul, heart, mind, and body.

I suppose my fifteen essays could stand alone, yet I must acknowledge that much of my nature-inspired learning and leading journey emerged from interactions with some amazing colleagues I've met along the way. As I prepared this second book, I accepted that my writing in isolation could not capture enough of the purpose and passion that drive and inspire me. I've included guest essays from five others who share my lifelong love of nature, thus enriching this book with their individual reflections. Their writing contributes elements that leverage my own observations and conclusions. I am grateful for their words, support, and stimulation. I'm pleased that Jeff Patnaude, Cary Keller, Ray Silverman, Bob Benton, and Jennifer Wilhoit accepted the challenge. Their belief in nature's inspiration for learning and leading buoys my confidence that we are on to something of merit. I am overwhelmed that others see value and substance in translating nature's wisdom and lessons to living, learning, serving, and leading.

I am humbled that they would embrace the concept and implore others to learn and apply these lessons. I met Jeff through a dear friend just a year ago, face-to-face, when Judy and I visited

Hesperides. We've admired and loved Cary since our days in Alaska. Ray emerged as friend and colleague during my Urbana University presidency; we share so much in life, nature, and Faith. Bob surfaced in my professional life since our move to the Tennessee Valley; he is helping me brand and market Great Blue Heron, LLC. We discovered that he has embraced the tenets and principles of nature-inspired learning and leading his entire adult life, without identifying it by any particular name. Jennifer is my only repeat guest essay author—my editor for the first book and this one, and fellow lessons-from-nature enthusiast.

I am deeply indebted to these five guest essayists, and to Cary Gaunt, my dear friend and colleague who I feel I have known for decades.

Entering the Zone of Courage

~ Choosing between courage and comfort ~

Once I knew that the shift to centralization at the system where I served as a campus president through June 2016 was certain and imminent, I began searching for a next presidency. I have now declared, six months after the central governing board announced elimination of all five campus presidents including me, that my search has ended. The system set me free, so to speak, less than three weeks before my sixty-fifth birthday. The fifteen applications I prepared and submitted were for CEO positions that started July 1, 2017, just 18 days prior to my reaching age sixty-six, and eligibility for full Social Security benefits.

Nearly all of the fifteen universities/colleges announced the same opportunity:

> "This is an exciting time at Acme College, presenting unparalleled opportunities for continued growth and transformation. Building on the exceptional work of the retiring president, Acme College offers its next president a distinctive and rich educational history, nationally recognized academic programs led by outstanding faculty, a strong financial position, a beautiful campus, a talented and committed community, and a close connection to one of the most dynamic cities in the country. Acme College's sound institutional foundation, coupled with its impressive

momentum, sets forth an outstanding leadership opportunity."

Who could resist the siren call? Change a few words here and there, and repeat the refrain for all fifteen. These institutions all sought the same person as well:

"Acme's next president will bring a highly relational approach, outstanding communication skills, authenticity, self-confidence balanced with humility, integrity of the highest order, a strong work ethic, and a clear understanding of higher education to her or his work. Acme seeks candidates who will embrace our distinctive nature and inspire faculty, students, staff, alumni, and trustees. Strong candidates will demonstrate the following skills, experiences, and characteristics:

- A visible leader interacting with various constituencies by actively engaging multiple perspectives on a residential campus, celebrating successes large and small, enthusiastically participating in the Acme College community, and favorably influencing the regional and national reputation of the College
- An inclusive leader with an understanding of and respect for Acme College's governance structure coupled with an abiding respect for the significant contributions of faculty
- A proven fundraiser…
- Student-centered and a tireless advocate for Acme's mission and core values
- A strategic visionary leader and planner with a proven ability to…
- An affirming team builder

- A person of financial acumen
- An energetic, optimistic, resilient leader with good humor who will provide respected, long-term leadership."

Again, alter a few words and it's the same special institution seeking the embodiment of an exemplary college/university CEO. I knew I was that person. I had tested myself under fire, and grown immeasurably in every engagement. Add the wisdom of my age, throw in disciplined physical fitness, peak mental acuity, emotional stability and strength, and a deep spiritual commitment. How could I miss? How could they refuse me? How would I decide among the choices? Each institution was perfect, for they had said so. I pulled out the atlas, weighed the pros and cons of the various locations, assessed which were within driving distance, near major airports, or no more than two flights from our grandchildren in Huntsville and Pittsburgh, and even checked out the climatological records. Where did we want to go? Where could we thrive? What might we tolerate for another five to ten years of steady income and great fringe benefits?

I learned, too, that they all write their rejection letters from the same template:

> "Dear Dr. Jones, I am writing with an update on the presidential search at Acme College. I am afraid I do not have positive news to share. Please know this was not a decision made lightly. Your materials received serious and thoughtful consideration, and there was much to admire about your candidacy. The competition in the pool is formidable with many seasoned leaders coming from top colleges and universities around the country. You were very well-regarded within this group of exceptional people."

Am I complaining? No, when I saw the language seeking "long-term leadership," I should have round-filed the position announcement, not bothering to prepare an application. I know it is illegal to discriminate on the basis of age but, really, I did the simple math. "Long-term" in my vernacular implies ten years or more. I also should have anticipated that the colleges and universities on my CEO portfolio do not position me among the candidates from top colleges and universities from around the country. Universities/colleges are ego-driven. "Ego-systems." I suppose I have been a working-class CEO at institutions far removed from the elite tier. But that is the track I have followed, with absolutely no regrets.

I am convinced that it's far easier to run an elite or upper tier institution. One heavily endowed, with assured gift and donation flow, a full complement of well-known faculty, a national or international reputation, well-maintained and palatial infrastructure, high-performing athletic teams, annual rewards for academics, service, and study abroad, and a deep bench of vice presidents, associate VPs, and executive directors of this and that. I wonder which is easier: paying a good mechanic and service center to maintain your Porsche, or rolling up your own sleeves and getting under the hood of your Plymouth Valiant? Both means of education do the trick: prepare future leaders, enable and inspire personal and professional development, and meet the country's growing need for citizens ready for life, work, and service. My hands may be a little more calloused, and my fingernails hold evidence of grease and labor. I don't require the trappings of an elite university. I know that every institution of higher education thinks itself a little better in many dimensions than it might be.

Zone of Comfort

I am who I am, and life has been good. I am not the least disturbed that the track did not lead to a fourth "permanent" presidency. In fact, I can celebrate receiving my fifteenth (and final) rejection! You might think that at age sixty-five I would know what was best for me, yet I have only slowly learned to trust and heed the judgment of those close to me. I listen, yet I still resist even the wisdom that my bride of many years offers. Since September 2015 when the general Antioch administration began signaling in not-so-subtle ways that the pendulum would swing full bore toward deeper centralization, Judy had observed, "You've had enough. We've had enough. You can't reverse the tide. You have talents that reach beyond leading an institution where forces beyond your control and outside your zone of reward and satisfaction prevail." Yet even then I began reviewing CEO position announcements and tossing my hat in a selected ring or two. Judy questioned my sanity.

Alas, I should have been more honest with myself. I admit now to feeling a little relief with each rejection, and great relief with the final one. I made it to two airport semi-finalist appearances and four semi-finalist video interviews, and felt some satisfaction. I knew that in each case I did my best. Several of the search firm reps said, "You did well, yet the *fit* wasn't right." "Fit" is an odd word. It's a catchall for "forgetaboutit." I have finally reached the point when I know I do not want another long-term college/university CEO position, another five-to-seven-year run. At this point, it is I who say "forgetaboutit"! I realize now that I was seeking comfort, security, a title, a familiar identity, and a steady income with benefits. More than forty-three years beyond my BS, I knew only one way to respond to the question nearly everyone asks upon first meeting, "What do you do?" I'm president, Antioch University New England. I lead Union Camp's forest fertilization research project. I'm a professor of forestry at Penn State. I'm Alabama Cooperative Extension Director.

I'm now struggling with a new answer, which I'll develop at the end of this essay. Judy and I have five grandchildren, two near us here in northern Alabama. I've created Great Blue Heron, LLC – Nature-Inspired Learning and Leading. I'm writing a great deal, and enjoying it. I'm focusing on my sweet spot. I've led three institutions of higher education, and mostly loved it. Our three years at Antioch University New England allowed greater alignment with that same sweet spot: graduate only; students enrolled to achieve a life-level transformation, an inflection in life's trajectory. I could focus on my own scholarship. I created the Nature Based Leadership Institute. Only when the pendulum began to swing inexorably toward centralization did the enjoyment and fulfillment wane.

All fifteen institutions to which I applied included major undergraduate facets: residence halls, athletics, and other elements beyond my sweet spot. Who was I kidding? I'm too old for another permanent presidency! The search committees nailed it. I was a lousy fit. The demands of every one of those long-term positions reached far beyond my yen and even my ken at this stage of life and career— the waning five-to-seven-years of serious professional pursuit.

My sweet spot occupied only some small percentage of the area circumscribed by the duties, responsibilities, and tasks demanded. My sweet spot overlaps fully with where I focus my writing, speaking, and consulting. I am whole, and I have just recently come to that conclusion. Judy has been telling me this for many months; she has shrugged and sighed with each and every application I submitted. She knows me better than I know myself.

I think I've now wrestled to the ground why it has taken me so long to see and accept. I know how to lead a university. I've learned a great deal through three such positions, much of it hard earned. I subscribe to a simple description of experience: it's that thing that you get right after you needed it. We don't learn by doing things correctly. The Antioch University New England presidency came so naturally for me. It felt so good, so right. I had mastered the craft by then, yet even that did not suffice given the centripetal force drawing operations to greater central control. Right place and right person; wrong time. I know now that what led me to crank out fifteen applications was my comfort with such positions. Another senior level role extending five-to-seven-years would keep me squarely in my zone of comfort, continuing to do what I know that I can. I have felt fear and trepidation about the specter of retirement, of doing something new and different, and venturing into new professional terrain.

Zone of Courage

Judy has been asking me for years, "Why don't you write more... you're good at it? You have done so much across the forest products industry and higher education. Why not tie it all together and do consulting?" Honestly?: I have been afraid of failure. I have pondered whether I am worthy of striking out more or less on my own. I have taken extended refuge in my Zone of Comfort. Multiple rejection letters have made it clear that I have outgrown, outlived, finding long-term refuge in that Zone of Comfort. Yet still I am bucking my own silent rebellion. What if nobody reads my writing? What if I hang the consulting shingle and my phone never rings? What if they laugh at my new garb? My disguise? What if they see me simply as the old retired guy, the one who has outlived his professional merit and worth?

However my entire professional career, Judy reminds me, I have always harbored self-doubt. Supervisors at Union Camp placed me in positions where the reach exceeded my grasp; they did it every time I attained some level of comfort in the current position. Their constant pushing and pulling ushered me through seven positions in three states across those 12 years. The same held true along my academic career track. Trusted friends and advisors encouraged me to apply for positions beyond my grasp. I suppose it's natural now to feel self-doubt once again.

> "Keep your face always toward the sunshine –
> and shadows will fall behind you."
> Walt Whitman

Judy and I have decided to face the sunshine, to once more push through my self-doubt. I've worked full time since May 1973. Even if nobody buys my book and no one hires me to consult, we won't find ourselves destitute. So, I must now enter the Zone of Courage, and we have decided to relish the thought. I've learned long ago that we do in fact choose such things. Relish, like so many such forces and attributes, is voluntary. Relish is an attitude. Great Blue Heron is accelerating into the Zone. My first book, "Nature Based Leadership," was released in December 2016. Nature-inspired learning and leading is my new realm; it defines and epitomizes my sweet spot. I find writing pleasurable. At the moment, I view it as an end, not necessarily a financial means. Writing forces (and enables) deep thinking.

I can conduct my affairs from our retirement home here on a small lake in Alabama's Tennessee River Valley, just three miles from our daughter and two of the grandkids. No more wishing I had more time to write. No more wondering whether the best years of my life are passing without permitting adequate time for shared sunsets, morning walks, continued dreaming, and relishing the quiet moments together.

I accept the Zone of Courage Challenge. I embrace this career capstone opportunity to live, learn, serve, and lead in the spirit of nature-inspired learning and leading, and to spread its gospel near and wide. I will devote my professional years of highest merit and best performance to Earth stewardship—to opening eyes through nature to encourage the four essential verbs in all that the people I reach do or might do: look, see, feel, and act. And to see and feel deeply through all five human portals: heart, mind; body; soul; and spirit.

I want my epitaph to read: He abandoned his Zone of Comfort; he ventured into a Zone of Courage; and he made the world a better place. He lived the gospel of nature-inspired learning and leading.

I'm now struggling with a new answer to the old question that people still ask, "What do you do?" Here's the answer—certainly gelling day by day—and still subject to further evolution and refinement. I am a retired university president. I am an evangelist and crusader for our human obligation to tinker with our one earth (and our only home) wisely. I aspire to be an intelligent tinkerer. I am a scholar advancing our understanding of humankind's essential relationship to Earth. I am an author translating my science through words that evoke comprehension, stir passion, elicit emotion, and prompt action. I am a consultant who brings purpose-driven, passion-fueled understanding to any entity willing to adopt nature-inspired learning and leading as a cornerstone for effective, positive, and profitable transformation.

In short, I have a new job. I am president and CEO of Great Blue Heron, LLC, a one-man show. I am GBH's lead scholar, principal author, primary consultant, and designated speaker. All that, and I am also husband, grandfather, birder, nature enthusiast, and grateful citizen of Planet Earth.

> "To keep every cog and wheel is the first precaution
> of intelligent tinkering."
> Aldo Leopold, Round River: From the Journals of Aldo Leopold

Chapter Endnote: I'm adding this text a full year after leaving Antioch University New England, and six months beyond drafting this essay. Great Blue Heron, LLC is now up and running. My second book (this one) will soon be published. I have not changed my mind about no longer seeking a long-term, permanent CEO position. However, at no point did I rule out the possibility of a special project that might engage me full time for a less-than-permanent position.

Such an opportunity presented itself three days before I received galley proofs from LifeRich Publishing. I accepted appointment as Interim President, Fairmont State University, a regional public university in northern West Virginia, not far from my western Maryland roots. An approximate six-month term, the position (again, not a permanent presidency) allows me to assist a university seeking the right experienced senior executive to bridge the university to exemplary permanent leadership in early 2018. I relish the opportunity to serve such an institution on an interim basis, even as I continue writing.

An interim presidency (within the spirit of a consulting contract), too, is new ground for me—territory that is both comfortable (leading a university) and courageous (what can I possibly do to enact change and mark progress in so short a span?). I have never before taken a position for the sole purpose of preparing to pass the leadership reigns near-term to a permanent successor.

So, I'm off to a new venture, one that falls within the Zone of Courage and exemplifies the spirit of new beginnings that sustains and inspires me.

Great Blue Heron, LLC

~ Paying forward the faith, confidence, and
wisdom of nature-inspired mentors ~

Last summer I created Great Blue Heron, LLC to apply my
expertise and experience in nature-inspired learning and
leading to institutions (from education to NGOs to business and
industry) seeking better performance and more effective, responsible
Earth stewardship. I am convinced that Great Blue Heron occupies
a unique niche: "Great Blue Heron operates at the intersection of
nature and human nature. We apply nature's wisdom to human-led
enterprises."

My web material text characterizes GBH's focus:

> "Great Blue Heron will give you full understanding
> of the limitless power of nature, and an appreciation
> for the spiritual dimension and essence of nature. We
> will show you, step by step, how to harness nature's
> wisdom and power, apply it to your enterprise, and
> achieve the triple bottom line you seek. We'll steer
> you toward channeling inspiration and humility,
> employing high purpose, full passion, and an intimate
> connection to Nature applicable to your enterprise.
> Great Blue Heron can infuse and inject nature's
> wisdom via direct consulting and coaching, inspiring
> presentations, mentoring, and workshop/seminar
> engagement, as well as with targeted writing."

I am writing my nature-inspired learning and leading book series under the banner of Great Blue Heron, LLC. Feeling the uncertainty of entering this new arena of semi-retirement and self-employment, I recently rationalized to a long-term colleague and friend: "The worst I can do is publish books nobody reads, maintain a web site that nobody opens, and offer services nobody purchases, and live on my retirement."

Hampshire Unit School, An Inaugural Project

My first assignment through Great Blue Heron, LLC came to me through my AUNE Nature Based Leadership Institute (NBLI) network. The timing could not have been better. Once more in my life and career, fortuity and serendipity have aligned uncannily. University of Tennessee Professor Mark Fly, one of the NBLI founders, invited my participation mid-August, 2016 in a project to reimagine a K-12 school in south-central Tennessee, near Columbia in Maury County. I immediately accepted the consulting gig, based just 85 miles up the road from my northern Alabama residence. Mark and I share a deep passion for improved K-12 and post-secondary education. Here is a thumbnail sketch, borrowing from our Hampshire project abstract:

> "We propose establishing a premier K-12 school (The Hampshire Unit School for Applied Science and Natural Resources (SAS&NR)) that can be a global exemplar. The SAS&NR will apply proven, effective elements of place-, project-, ag-, and nature-based learning from kindergarten through 12th grade, and across the curriculum. The School will operate at the intersection of theory and practice, and will exemplify a spirit of learning and education that is purpose-driven and passion-fueled. The SAS&NR will emerge as a true feeder school—one so good that parents will ache to *feed* their children into it. A school

so effective that employers, community colleges/
technical schools, and universities want to *feed* from
its graduate pool. A school that reciprocally establishes
articulation agreements with other education entities.
The SAS&NR will be a *community school*, engaging
effectively with Maury County citizens, businesses,
not-for-profits, and government."

The School (teachers, staff, parents), the county commissioners,
the county school board, the principal, superintendent, and many
other Hampshire stakeholders have embraced the notion and dream
of a globally significant school. A summer 2016 transformation task
force led the way. I entered the picture in early September at an all-day
teacher professional development session devoted to bringing life to
the transformation. Later that month, I sat with the superintendent,
the two lead county commissioners, Dr. Fly, the school board chair,
and other lead participants in the school gymnasium. We interacted
with some 200 keenly interested and engaged parents, citizens, and
students. The atmosphere might best have been characterized as
charged with energy, yet tinged with some natural concerns and
worries. I've been up many times since then, meeting with multiple
parties who want to engage.

We've fine-tuned the existing Hampshire Unit School mission
and vision only slightly to embody the focused Hampshire SAS&NR
approach:

"Mission: Integrate agricultural and nature-based
sciences throughout the core curriculum in a
nurturing environment, created and maintained by
a high level of parent and community involvement.

Vision: Applied agricultural and nature-based sciences
are conducive to powerful learning; technology and
hands-on experiences, along with real-world (project,
place, and nature) problem solving in all subjects,

> will increase motivation, relevance, and achievement
> for our students, as well as prepare and empower all
> students for lifelong success in a changing world."

One example of the concerns that some stakeholders have is that our curricular emphasis on the natural sciences will ignore the needs of and poorly serve students who might otherwise be drawn to health sciences, business, teaching, and other fields. Our response is that the focus is broader in reach; the Hampshire SAS&NR will embody a learning methodology that will stimulate learning *across* the curriculum. Importantly, the Hampshire SAS&NR will provide an education platform that will inspire and enable: better learners and thinkers (now and lifelong); citizens (informed, inspired, and engaged); workers (from agriculture to law to health sciences to business to crafts and trade); and leaders (in any arena where they might serve). Students and graduates will drink deeply and enthusiastically of disciplines far beyond agriculture, natural resources, and the environment; the latter are the means, not the end.

Increasingly, the education literature makes a convincing case for the efficacy of learning that is experiential, hands-on, and problem-, project-, and place-based. Maury County provides a location ideally suited to centering such a focused curriculum on nature-inspired learning, incorporating the region's current and historical rich natural environment and its vibrant agricultural economy. David Sobel, Richard Louv, Cheryl Charles, and many others write compellingly of the power of nature-inspired learning. Hampshire SAS&NR will model an approach that will yield desired results.

I view nature, in all its various dimensions and applications, as a project-rich learning environment across the curriculum, whether English, math, sociology, life and physical sciences, philosophy, business, or the arts. Nature is an ideal medium and setting for inspired thinking, learning, and practice. Maury County is fertile with nature in all its dimensions and splendor.

I cannot imagine a better way than engaging with the Hampshire School to establish Great Blue Heron, LLC, whose tagline reads:

"nature-inspired learning and leading; applying nature's wisdom to life and work." Such could just as well be the tagline for the Hampshire SAS&NR. We have an opportunity to test my hypothesis that every lesson for living, learning, serving, and leading is either written compellingly *in,* or is powerfully inspired *by* nature.

An Integrated Lifespan Service Center: Living and Aging with Grace, Fulfillment, Joy, Dignity, and Purpose

The second GBH client is a woman of color who owns a senior care enterprise. She is a truly amazing, force-of-nature, rock star-level entrepreneur. I am working with her to define and realize her dream for enabling living and aging with grace, fulfillment, joy, dignity, and purpose. The goal statement for the project is: "Envision, define, and realize The Dream to create a globally significant, integrated lifespan service center in Alabama's Tennessee Valley region. The owner understands, appreciates, and embraces the core philosophy at the center of GBH's purpose: that nature can and must be central to such a vision.

The Great Blue Heron approach is applicable to diverse enterprises. A K-12 school and an elder care center may at first glance appear to have little in common, yet both focus on adding value to life and instilling a deeper appreciation for our place in the world. Both clients, and all those I hope to reach, can gain from the Great Blue Heron practice and philosophy. All enterprises benefit from removing the blinders that too often distract from purpose and action.

Great Blue Heron, LLC's Four Essential Verbs

Through Great Blue Heron, I want to help individuals, enterprises (for-profit and social-profit), communities, governmental entities, and schools to better serve their constituents, employees, citizens, communities, and students. I see a real need to open eyes; far too many people traipse blindly through their daily existence, oblivious to the beauty, magic, wonder, and awe of the world around them.

I recall decades ago as a distance runner seeing others logging their miles, totally cut off by their ear bud cacophony from spring birdsong, trees dripping morning fog, the breeze in roadside vegetation, their own breath and cadenced heart, and even pleasant greetings from fellow runners. Today many people see little more than the digital glow from their handheld devices, distracting them from tranquil surroundings and assigning false urgency and importance to the most mundane, insignificant, and rote of matters. I see it as akin to striking life's knife-edge across a blunting surface, dulling the blade to ineffectiveness.

Great Blue Heron adopts and proffers the belief that imposed, accepted, and too often embraced blindness to the world around us detracts and disables our ability, desire, and zeal for achievement. It is both agent and artifact of failing to look. Blindness of the kind I speak derives first from not bothering to look. And, without first looking, how can we ever hope to see? My rationale is both circular and self-fulfilling. *Look* is the first of four essential verbs for truly experiencing life in its multiple dimensions. Looking entails far more than an occasional glance up from the digital depths; that barest glimpse may avoid head-on collisions of opposing digitally-engaged pedestrians. But it does not enable one to truly *see*, as Henry David Thoreau knew: "It's not what you look at that matters, it's what you see."

Seeing requires more than a superficial recognition of objects, people, and places. Great Blue Heron encourages people to see deeply, beyond the superficial to the depths of dimension, nuance, and meaning. Seeing is about more than vision. Seeing is how we examine our way of living, learning, serving, and leading. Seeing, in this case, is a metaphor for employing the full spectrum of our senses. Seeing is the vehicle through which we absorb our surroundings, each tuned and practiced: mind, body, heart, soul, and spirit. Thoreau intended just that. He experienced and wrote about nature in dimensions removed from his eyesight. In that interpretation, most of us see so very little. He continued: "We live but a fraction of our lives."

Great Blue Heron implores an approach that recognizes the limits of looking and seeing. I believe—and Great Blue Heron espouses, coaches, and counsels—that we must see deeply enough to stimulate empathy to the point that we *feel*. Looking and seeing without feeling provides little more return than a topical treatment; it falls far short of salve for our souls. Both Thoreau and his contemporary John Muir knew the dividends of feeling: "I took a walk in the woods and came out taller than the trees." (Thoreau) "In every walk with nature one receives far more than he sees." (Muir)

Finally, Great Blue Heron admonishes that looking, seeing, and feeling fail to reach an end that makes a difference for a better tomorrow. We must explore feelings deep enough to stimulate, motivate, and inspire us to *act*.

My goal is to embody the four essential verbs as guiding tenets for Great Blue Heron, LLC and its gospel of nature-inspired learning and leading. My *modus operandi* is to implore that every enterprise consciously practice the art of looking, seeing, feeling, and acting. Success and achievement, both personally and professionally, demand it.

GBH's Core Values

Great Blue Heron assists enterprises and individuals who are anchored in personal integrity and professional ethics. GBH will also help enterprises and individuals understand and embrace environmental stewardship and selfless service, if those two essential values are not already at the center of the endeavor. The core values I espouse are:

- Responsible earth stewardship. All enterprises are citizens of Planet Earth. GBH works with those who accept and embrace, or are willing to open their eyes to this fundamental value.
- Intelligent tinkering. This value is ecosystem based. We must recognize that all things are interconnected and

interdependent. We must know the consequences and implications of all actions.

- Doing good by doing well. This value recognizes our obligation to the greater good now and into the deep future. It involves performing well enough to give back and pay forward. Great Blue Heron works only with enterprises that accept such an obligation for doing good.
- Sustainability. Leaving a world that can provide a future undiminished from the one we occupy, recognizing that we have an obligation to future generations.
- Triple Bottom Line. Making a financial profit is necessary, yet not sufficient. GBH helps clients understand the environmental and social bottom lines in addition to the financial. Our clients want to achieve net profit along all three bottom lines.
- Four levels of fitness. GBH helps leaders recognize the critical nature of their own four-dimensional fitness, even as they understand that capacity and performance correlate with employee health and wellbeing. Great Blue Heron helps clients understand that maintaining fitness in these four areas enhances their ability to perform as well as draw satisfaction and fulfillment from their efforts to achieve fitness.
  - o Mental – acuity and sharpness
  - o Physical – health and vitality
  - o Emotional – friends, families, colleagues
  - o Spiritual – embrace of a presence larger than self
- Employing all five portals. A GBH client appreciates the need to operate and thrive along the wholeness of human experience: through mind, body, heart, soul, and spirit. Life and work are not one-dimensional.

Earn This!

A handful of remarkable mentors and personal and professional heroes have shaped me over the years. To them I owe much. They include my dad; Dr. Jack Berglund, SUNY ESF Professor and my Ph.D. adviser (Jack died two years into my three-year program); Dr. William Johnson, also then a faculty member at ESF, now deceased; Dr. Robert C. Kellison, forest products industry consultant and NC State professor, and still dear friend; "Doc" Glenn Workman, my junior college professor and still lifetime friend; as well as others. Through Great Blue Heron, I want and intend to pay forward their deep investment (of time, talent, wisdom, and confidence) in me. I feel genuine humility thinking that I can somehow be worthy. They are giants in so many dimensions.

At the end of the movie, "Saving Private Ryan," the dying Captain Miller who led the mission implores Private Ryan (for whom several soldiers have made the ultimate sacrifice during the extended daring rescue) to "earn this." At the movie's end, an aged Ryan returns to the military cemetery, collapsing and sobbing at the captain's cross, offering respect, gratitude, and the faint hope that perhaps his life has been worthy. I recently watched the movie again, and felt the same deep resonance. I can only hope that I have earned the love, interest, and faith my mentors gave to me. It is with palpable humility that I dare to create Great Blue Heron, LLC in the spirit of the memory of my deceased mentors and in honor of those still living.

How can I act and perform in a manner worthy of their faith in me? That is one of my challenges. Can I rise to their silent, yet implied exhortations that I "earn this"? I will not simply look for success. I intend to be too busy to do other than see, feel, and act. I have said for years that one of my primary frustrations with the higher education world is its tendency to encourage learning that stops short of equipping students for good action in the world. Therefore, I intend to focus Great Blue Heron on action. My mentors and heroes walked the talk, demonstrating through their actions a deep commitment and embrace of what I now call Nature Based Leadership. I am grateful for them laying the cornerstones for Great Blue Heron, LLC.

Dad passed away during my Penn State faculty years. He cared little about my career accomplishments, though he expressed his pride in those markers. He loved me as only a father loves a son: without judgment of achievement. Dr. Johnson passed before I left the forest products industry to pursue the doctoral degree. Jack Berglund died while I administered CPR, still a year away from earning my Ph.D. Of the five of these I honor, only Doc Workman and Bob Kellison remain. Wonderfully and magnificently, they care (as did those now deceased) more about Judy and me, our wellbeing, than any career peaks or valleys. They gave selflessly to me for reasons other than thinking one day I might be a university president or start a consulting business. Perhaps paying it forward is hardwired in human nature? Perhaps we invest ourselves where we see promise and potential because doing so may best ensure species' sustainability. Perhaps we throw ourselves into those within whom we see some reflection or echo of ourselves, thus surfacing a bit of self-preservation. Whatever the motivation, the trait is admirable.

Have I likewise invested in others across my own mid and later years? I take comfort that I can name a few. Have I paid forward the guidance, faith, and wisdom Jack, Doc, Bob, and the others offered to me? Until my last breath, I shall commit to continued reinvestment. I shall strive to be worthy. I shall carry the banner high for nature-inspired learning and leading!

The Law of Attraction

A Guest Essay by Bob Benton

I know this book can change lives and I want to share why I believe this to be so. The law of attraction brought me to be friends with a kindred spirit who happens to be the author of this book: Steve Jones. We quickly discovered that we share the same love, reverence, and respect for nature. Like Steve, nature taught me lessons for life that have enabled me to walk a path of faith, accomplishment, joy, and fulfillment.

On the surface I am just another professional man with some gray hair. And just like most of today's professionals, I am part of the digital age. But I have an advantage over my younger counterparts. I am a baby boomer. I grew up without computer games, cell phones, or social media. My playground was Mother Nature. My imagination was a limitless toy box from which I created games and fantasy worlds. My social life was robust and real. My many friends were not on Facebook or Twitter, but my band of brothers who shared my love for nature and adventure. In short, I was born in an analog world and migrated into to the digital world. I was connected deeply to Mother Nature before I connected to technology. I am as strong as any oak tree, as flexible and powerful as any river, as keen as a Great Blue Heron, and solid as a rock. I am connected to the limitless power and wisdom of nature, and the universal, eternal energy of God. My lifelong understanding of this reality has allowed me to live a life of fulfillment, success, and joy, both personally and professionally.

Unfortunately, countless others are powerless, fearful, and

unhappy. Far too many people see only the superficial world. They are blind and deaf to the unseen riches and power that is nature. Instead, they seek satisfaction and fulfillment in materials trappings. They are like a dog that chases its tail. And ironically, the harder they work to find satisfaction, the more it eludes them. I know personally that there is no real value in the material world. Thoreau sums up my heartfelt empathy for the tail-chasers with this quote: "Most men lead lives of quiet desperation and die with their song still inside them."

My hope is that the law of attraction will put this book into the millions of hands that so dearly need to grasp it.

Bio

Bob Benton is a national award-winning practitioner of multi-sensory branding. His decades of experience in turning companies into brands have won him many national and regional awards. He is one of the pioneers of neuro-marketing. His deep understanding of neuroscience, coupled with behavioral psychology, enables him to craft authentic brands that connect on the all-important emotional level. His clients include, but are not limited to, American Express, Avnet, Microsoft, NASA, Dow Chemical, NASA, Whitman's Chocolates, C&H Sugar, Boeing, and Interfuze.

Hesperides: Wisdom Center for Inner Excellence

~ Every setting (natural and otherwise) is an island in the stream of life ~

Judy and I visited the Wisdom Center for Inner Excellence on April 6 and 7, 2016. I offer my reflections and observations from what we hope is the first of many such sojourns. The WCIE promises to open eyes, heart, mind, soul, and spirit to the wonder, beauty, awe, and magic that lie within each participant who enters the WCIE realm. The experience will motivate all to really look, truly see, deeply feel, and consciously act to better ourselves as well as the world in which we live, learn, serve, and lead.

Island in the Sky

Mount Marshall stands 3,368 feet tall, a sentinel along the northern Blue Ridge. It is prominent from our Wisdom Center sun porch view to the WSW across the fields. Our perch atop Viewtree Mountain (1,050 feet) sits 500 feet above and a couple of miles west of Warrenton, Virginia, accessed via Hesperides Road's multiple switchbacks climbing from Bear Wallow Road. Twelve line-of-sight miles from us, Marshall's nearly one-half-mile vertical advantage draws our view. While spring's green graces Viewtree's hilltop yellow poplars, we can see that the verdant colors reach only Marshall's lower slopes.

Neighboring Mount Marshall may outrank us, yet every topographic feature east of Viewtree to the coast lies vertically subordinate. We stand alone. Last evening's southeasterly winds raked our promontory, the first significant barrier across hundreds of miles of coastal plain and piedmont fetch. The wind seemed delighted with the Viewtree challenge. As we descended the old logging trail through the east side forest, the persistent summit gusts quickly subsided to a gentle breeze as we descended. The gale remained above us. Even from Bear Wallow Road we could hear the ridge top torrents. I suppose the wind saw no need to torment the lower slopes; she had spring work to do delivering warm wet greetings to points north, including my then-home in New Hampshire. Just two days earlier, winds from another direction (and a prior season) blanketed our New England home with more than half a foot of snow.

Viewtree Mountain was an island in that evening's river of air rushing to the north. Imagine turbulence around rocks in a tumbling stream; we overnighted on the rock, the air frothing around the buildings and through the gusty yellow poplars, oaks, walnuts, and white pine. The wind rose occasionally to 40 miles per hour. However, more importantly, it was helping propel spring northward.

Through these transition seasons spring advances at some 100 miles (or 800 vertical feet) per week. Solar incidence and sun angle assist, complement, and magnify the wind. Keene, NH, is four seasonal progression weeks north of Warrenton; my near-Keene house was at 900 feet elevation and measured nine inches of snow the Sunday and Monday prior to our Wednesday hike. Marshall Mountain, with its vertical superiority, lags three seasonal weeks behind the center, hence its green-deprived upper slopes and summit.

What led me to the center? A dear mutual friend and colleague brought Judy and me together with the center's founders on this midweek overnight sandwiched between two three-day transformational leadership workshops. We intended to delve deeply into whether the center might find incremental value by more mindfully and intentionally adopting and incorporating elements of nature-inspired learning and leading. Founder Jeff Patnaude and I did just that, stimulated in part by our Wednesday afternoon stroll through field and forest. We wandered and wondered. Jeff's education and lifelong practice focused on mind, heart, soul, and spirit. My training and much of my experience found me in nature, deeply influenced by—and oriented to—the environment. Both of us found application and lessons in our respective immersions for living, learning, serving, and leading. Hence, our worlds swung into mutual orbit and resonance.

Transformational leadership here at the center operates in a human dimension, embedded in its physical setting, across time, proceeding inexorably at 60 minutes per hour. Aldo Leopold saw the invisible applications of nature to living and observed,

> "Like winds and sunsets, wild things were taken for granted until progress began to do away with them. Now we face the question whether a still higher 'standard of living' is worth its cost in things natural, wild, and free. For us of the minority, the opportunity to see geese is more important than television."

I subscribe to the truth that we must deeply see the multiple dimensions in which we live, learn, serve, and lead—see them through the lens that is nature based. How many of Jeff's dedicated workshop participants measure the passage of the seasons, or even of time, in miles of latitude or vertical feet per week? How many are blind to the natural world? Can they expect to see within themselves if so much of the outer world lies hidden or obscured? What else are participants missing?

Feathered Friends and Fellow Viewtree Inhabitants

I saw no bird feeders or nesting boxes atop the Center's Viewtree Mountain paradise. I thought again of Leopold, "One swallow does not make a summer, but one skein of geese, cleaving the murk of a March thaw, is the spring." I wondered how workshop and retreat participants might truly engage and immerse in their Blue Ridge foothill mental, emotional, and leadership retreat without having a sense of the harbingers that ride the spring winds northward, in some cases, from thousands of miles into Central and South America.

I pondered how workshop participants at WCIE could possibly comprehend their fleeting and fragile place in this world without knowing what fellow Earth inhabitants—without benefit of technology and with body mass no greater than a few grams—risk to fully advantage their brief avian breeding season in far northern latitudes. The tools of survival, sustainability, and fecundity are written by eons of striving, learning, and recording; their DNA is rich with lessons learned.

I urged Jeff over predawn coffee Thursday to consider adding another dimension to his ridge top curriculum. Erect some bird feeders and keep them filled; place a few nesting boxes around the property. Install a few outdoor microphones and pipe the music of joyous feathered migrants and residents into the gathering spaces at the center. Jeff so eloquently quoted to me over our second cup of coffee, "Faith is the bird's predawn voice, assuring us that once again today, the eastern sky will soon brighten." Leadership is in part faith; even the birds know this! Why waste the wisdom of nature at a center that occupies an island in the stream of life? Employ nature's ways. Otherwise, we just as well house participants at an airport hotel: let them leaf through nature photography books, show them some beautiful nature videos, read a few relevant quotes, and send them on their way.

If instead, they come to the island, I implore that we immerse them in every sense of the term. Don't waste a moment or miss an opportunity. Birds—especially our intrepid, intercontinental migratory friends—bring deep instruction and inspiration. What rich return on an investment in a few hundred pounds of seed and the labor to keep the feeders stocked! Add a score of nesting boxes across the ridge top, and chronicle the tale of life and renewal on the island. Our intention underlying the addition of feeders and nesting boxes is to attract these fellow Earth citizens to the center, to ensure that our human guests witness firsthand our place *in* nature, not apart from it. The purpose is not to feed the migrating birds who are quite capable of sustaining themselves, but to feed and fuel the hungry souls and intellect of center participants.

We can welcome these feathered friends to our daytime lives at the center, and observe them firsthand. Our nocturnal neighbors will generally, with the exception of a rare daytime sighting, remain beyond our experience. However, we can bring even these into view with a handful of strategically placed trail cameras, triggered in darkness by the nighttime wanderers. Digitally recorded at the center, the images every morning will further demonstrate that we are not alone. We are never truly alone. Let the Wisdom Center for Inner Excellence remind us of our inter- and inner-dependence in all that we do.

On a stroll, we neared the eastern end of the hilltop meadow and saw an immature bald eagle lift from its tree perch at the edge of the field. It was carried into the wind with strong and confident wing strokes, passing over and beyond the woods. We reveled at its appearance, wishing it had soared and lingered a bit longer. Had we not ventured into the field, and instead stuck to the paved access road, we would not have seen this magnificent young avian predator. I had suggested the woods route, fully anticipating that we would see more in this deeper immersion into the outdoors. Exploring nature and its lessons is a contact sport. Likewise, living, learning, serving, and leading work best in full and positive contact, face-to-face and shoulder-to-shoulder.

The Forest's Story

The forest we entered tells its story willingly to those who can comprehend its language. Nearly forty-four years beyond my forestry bachelor's degree and three decades since earning a doctorate in natural resources management, I can read and speak the language fluently; though I admit to some rustiness from the twenty years since I left my almost daily woodsy classrooms and laboratories! The tales are poignant and compelling. For example, the logging trail and scattered cut stumps, now weathered and decaying, signal the timber harvesting from nearly ten years ago. Amazingly, the canopy gaps from tree removal have already filled, testament to the remaining trees' hunger to reach for more sunlight by extending branches into the temporarily sun-filled openings. Hence, the demonstrated meaning and merit to the old saw, "Nature abhors a vacuum."

A little farther to the east and downslope we intersect many former main canopy trees lying prostrate, as northerly winds tossed them toward the south, root balls lifted from the then-moist soil. The derecho that tore them from the ground several summers ago had already traveled hundreds of miles before leaving its Viewtree calling card. Now, nature will once more fill the canopy voids, even as the downed branches and wood reenter and enrich the soil that nurtures the survivors. Evolution assures that those remaining know what to do, how to exploit the blessed incremental sun energy and supplemental soil nutrition. Any enterprise should anticipate and prepare to mine advantages and opportunities, both those that are anticipated as well as those that are unseen.

Cursory examination would lead one to conclude that the life (the emerging green), death (the blow-down and other woody debris scattered across the forest floor), and dynamics of the forest (leaves, nuts, and other annual deposits) occur where we look and see, walk, and appreciate. However, even with all the clear above-ground evidence, fully seventy-five percent of forest carbon turnover is subsurface, occurring out of sight, where the vibrant cycles and streams of life rev and teem year-round. Fine roots, mycorrhizal fungi, and tiny flora and fauna constitute a thriving stew. Never a dull moment, even when the above-ground life sleeps under the Virginia winter's occasional deep snow and sub-freezing periods. The lesson: so much in life, business, and even our individual lives, lies hidden. The real and essential functions are evident only to those who know where to look and what to seek.

As with any enterprise, nothing in the seeming timeless woods is static; nothing stands still. Even ancient forests are finite. The huge yellow poplars lining the center's moist and fertile concave slopes, the most favorable tree-growing environments on the property, are at least second growth. These fertile Blue Ridge foothills have been cleared, some more than once since colonial settlement. Man clears; nature reclaims. Of course, humans are not the only agent of forest removal. Derechos, massive coastal storms, thick ice, wildfires, and many other natural agents of forest disturbance have operated across the eons. Forests are prepared for man-caused disturbance because forest perturbation is natural. It predates humans' arrival in North America; forest disturbance occurred for millennia before Homo sapiens evolved on this fine Earth. Nothing is static; nothing stays the same. With careful study, we can resurrect a deeper story of the center's land history: a task for a subsequent visit.

We observed spring ephemerals in full flower (cutleaf toothwort, Virginia pussytoes, purple violet, may-apple, rue anemone, and others) exploiting the early season warmth in the nearly full sunlight available before the tree canopy leafed out. These opportunists complete their seasonal life cycle when they can, hence the term "spring ephemerals." Ecclesiastes nailed it, "To every thing there is a season, and a time to every purpose under heaven." Lessons learned are available only to those who look and see. Other lessons claim their own season. The circuit we walked offers chapters that ebb and flow seasonally and across time, year after year.

Walnuts, acorns, hickory nuts, maple samaras, poplar seeds, and many other signs and signals litter the ground; they speak volumes and fill long passages of lively prose. Deer trails, fresh scat, buck rubs, "bird peck" on hickories, fungal fruiting bodies, tree stem cavities, and other ubiquitous evidence are there to those able and eager to see and discern. The lessons are easily interpreted, and imminently decipherable to those who know the natural tongues and observable syntax. One route to inner excellence passes through interconnectedness to the world we inhabit and the nature that sustains us.

Nature's Role in Jeff's WCIE Vision

Just 48 miles from our nation's capital, the center welcomes transformational leaders and mentors to contemplate and learn ways to change the world; this is Jeff's vision. Their journey toward a fulfilling and rewarding life begins long before they reach Viewtree Mountain. They come because they realize that the hilltop immersion avails them an inflection point, a gateway through which to seek inner excellence. The gateway triggers an awakening to the natural world that sustains, nurtures, humbles, and inspires. The experience at WCIE motivates all who pass through the Viewtree Mountain world to really look, truly see, deeply feel, and consciously act to better ourselves and the world in which we live, learn, serve, and lead.

There is palpable wisdom in the woods: powered by the ages and reinforced by the ebbs and flows of energy, life, and seasons. Our fellow journeyers (human, other fauna, and flora) enrich our lives and accompany our own passage through time and space. Our inner examination returns dividends only when we also focus outwardly, and understand and appreciate the world around us, manmade and natural. And what better place to ensure bridging internal to external than this special wind stream island, which Jeff describes in Celtic terms as a "thin place," an environment where Heaven and Earth intersect. Judy and I felt the "thin-ness." Countless leaders have as well.

Nature offers lessons for those willing to pay attention and to behave in accordance with what they have learned. Nature based leadership examines how leaders can learn from nature's lessons. I am excited by the prospect of partnering professionally with the WCIE at a "thin place" just 48 miles from Washington D.C. The landscape beckons, offering exquisite elements for integrating nature's lessons with inner discovery and exploration. Nature-inspired learning and leading workshops, intensives, and courses delivered onsite at WCIE will provide easy access and the perfect environment for participants from the DC area, and from across the globe.

Aldo Leopold's *A Sand County Almanac* offers fitting closure to these reflections:

"A March morning is only as drab as he who walks in it without a glance skyward, ear cocked for geese. I once knew an educated lady, banded by Phi Beta Kappa, who told me that she had never heard or seen the geese that twice a year proclaim the revolving seasons to her well-insulated roof. Is education possibly a process of trading awareness for things of lesser worth?"

Awareness of nature and our place within nature adds greater worth to living, learning, serving, and leading. Nature-inspired learning and leading instruct us that life is best experienced when we do not stick to the paved access road. Find escape occasionally from the stifling suffocation of a well-insulated roof. Insist upon a literal and metaphorical glance skyward, ear cocked for geese.

The Tree of Life

~ Our lives are directed by heritage;
mine orients me to trees, and through
trees, to nature and Earth ~

F riend and colleague Jeff Patnaude, Wisdom Center for Inner
Excellence, sent me a brief passage last year from The Revelation;
he had heard it in church that morning.

"The leaves of the tree are for the healing of the nations."

Jeff knows I am a forester. I had walked the center's heavily-
forested property with Jeff just a few weeks prior. He knew I would
appreciate the message for its literal and symbolic meanings, observing
that it, "is a lovely item to ponder."

I acknowledged Jeff's message later that afternoon. His note
prompted me to do a bit of research. I found the following with a
little exploration on the Internet:

From the King James version of the Bible:

> "In the midst of the street of it, and on either side of
> the river, was there the tree of life, which bare twelve
> manner of fruits, and yielded her fruit every month: and
> the leaves of the tree were for the healing of the nations."

And from the Book of Ezekiel, also in the King James Bible:

> "And by the river upon the bank thereof, on this side
> and on that side, shall grow all trees for meat, whose

leaf shall not fade, neither shall the fruit thereof be consumed: it shall bring forth new fruit according to his months, because their waters they issued out of the sanctuary: and the fruit thereof shall be for meat, and the leaf thereof for medicine."

And from gotQuestions.org, in answer to "what is the tree of life":

"The tree of life, referred to in Genesis, is the symbol of God's provision for immortality in the Garden of Eden. Of all the trees that were in the Garden of Eden, two were named for their great importance, but just as one—the tree of life—was a blessing, to Adam and Eve, the other was to become a curse for all of their posterity"

From Genesis to Revelation, the tree of life provides for God's children. It's sad that more than two millennia later the teeming masses seem blind to our dependence upon the literal and metaphorical tree of life, the one Earth whose bounty sustains us. I suggest that the spiritual tree of life that reveals itself through our five portals (mind, body, heart, soul, and spirit) likewise feeds and nourishes us, even as its leaves have the magic and power to heal all nations, if only we open our eyes to our fleeting and fragile place along the river of life.

Joyce Kilmer saw the simple beauty and elegance in trees:

"I think that I shall never see, A poem lovely as a tree. A tree whose hungry mouth is prest, Against the sweet earth's flowing breast; Poems are made by fools like me, But only God can make a tree."

Kilmer's is not the tree of life, the rich source of sustenance for God's children. His tree is the symbol of life dependent upon our one earth. He depicts the earth as provider, the Mother. Kilmer implies that words are empty, that nature (God) instead is the essence. He suggests that ultimate goodness derives from the Earth. I believe Kilmer is reminding us of our humility before nature, that we are merely fools to think we can best a tree. I think, too, that he saw trees as inspiration, a work of incredible art, and symbol of our need to thank a higher power for the tree and all of nature's bounty: "A tree that looks at God all day, and lifts her leafy arms to pray."

Throughout my career in forestry people have often introduced me as a "tree guy." That's shorthand, I suppose, for forester. And I much prefer that characterization over "forest ranger." I've never been a forest ranger. A forest ranger in my experience is not necessarily credentialed with a four-year, hard-science bachelor's degree. A forest ranger is often the person employed by a federal or state agency to monitor and respond to fires or other threats to the forest. A forest ranger is usually a technician, not a professional forester. The ranger also enforces applicable state laws and regulations with respect to hunting, fishing, camping, and firewood cutting. A common misperception is that a forester works in a fire tower, but that is actually within the scope of the ranger job. Perhaps it's a matter of professional pride or smugness that I insist that I am a forester; I never worked as a ranger.

While a forester can be a forest ranger, forestry is a profession that begins with an undergraduate degree in forestry. A forester is a professional who practices the art and science of forestry. A forester's range of duties and responsibilities encompasses ecological restoration, timber harvesting, prescribed burning, forest planning, tree planting, site preparation, forest protection, and myriad other daily and long term forest management activities and functions. The profession of forestry has expanded since my BS conferral and now includes: carbon sequestration, wetlands mitigation, global positioning, biodiversity management, as well as other dimensions spurred by increased population growth and technological advances.

Trees and forests propelled me to my 1973 BS degree in forestry. I've enjoyed a lifelong love affair with trees. Growing up in the central Appalachian Mountains, my recreational life centered around hiking, camping, hunting, and fishing among those biologically diverse mixed-hardwood forests. During those formative years, I intuitively understood that trees drew lifeblood from the soil, yet I did not make the poetic leap to trees suckling at earth's breast. Although now, I'm particularly fond of Kilmer's tree "whose hungry mouth is prest against the sweet earth's flowing breast." I had not made the following connection until this very moment as I compose this essay.

Ironically, I devoted four years of my private sector forestry career to tree nutrition and forest fertilization research across the six southeastern states (VA, NC, SC, GA, FL, and AL). Researching how we might sweeten and amend "the mother's milk" to economically produce more and higher quality wood beyond the capacity of the non-amended soil. When I left the company to work toward my doctorate, circumstances aligned for my dissertation topic to examine the relationship between soil/site and forest productivity. I assessed the quality of Earth's sweet flowing breast based upon soil/site factors such as: aspect (the direction a slope faces); percent slope; position on the slope (upper, mid, and lower); slope shape (concave, flat, or convex); soil depth; soil texture; soil chemistry; relative shading from nearby hills; and other measurable factors.

The quality of Mother's nectar varies, I found, with those critical soil/site characters. Where the tree suckles makes a big difference. The Earth's capacity to nourish is not uniform. The tree's ability to grow to its potential depends upon where it is situated. The soil provides moisture, nutrients, aeration, microbial chemical sources, and anchorage. The roots, stems, and conductive tissue transport the raw materials of life to the leaves: the tree's factories. Those engines of production convert sunlight, water, and carbon dioxide to simple sugars: the building blocks for the meat of the fruit and the medicine for the healing of nations.

The Bible is rich with parables from nature, even as oral histories across the world speak to our dependence upon nature. Are we forgetting these lessons from human history at a time when we are most vulnerable to irreversible human impact on the nature that sustains us? I fear that we are. The tree of life is symbol for the very earth that feeds, clothes, shelters, heals, and inspires us. Earth is the tree of life. We risk destroying inexorably that upon which we depend. We have the means to diminish this earth—its soil, flora, fauna, and climate—in ways that will lessen our ability to live sustainably. In many ways, the Earth itself is the tree of the knowledge of good and evil. Each day we consume more and more of the forbidden fruit. We are the serpent. Our ignorant, satanic treatment of Mother Earth may be exacting our own demise. Two thousand years ago, sage humans knew the parables for a sustainable future. We ignore the laws of nature at our own peril. Nature based and nature-inspired learning and leading remind us of our own limits, counsel us to pay heed to the wisdom of the ages.

Trees literally provide food, shelter, and habitat for creatures large and small, for flora from resurrection fern to mistletoe to lichens and algae, as well as for squirrels, birds, snakes, and other critters. Trees extend life above the horizontal to a three-dimensional reality that enlivens and enriches the life zone. Collectively, trees compose the forests of life, the wonderful series of ecosystems that cover so much of the world I have inhabited across 65 years and 12 states: from Georgia's piney woods, to the Appalachian mixed mesophytic forests, to New England's northern hardwoods, to Alaska's taiga. My four-acre parcel in southwest New Hampshire comprised at least eleven main canopy species (red and white oak, white and black birch, black cherry, aspen, red and sugar maple, hickory, white pine, and hemlock). The woods are vibrant with life, all derived from the complex interrelationships powered by sunlight, water, carbon dioxide, simple sugars, and nutrients.

The earth *and* the living creatures dependent upon it are what comprise the tree of life. We humans represent the only living conscience of Earth stewardship. It is only we who have the power to destroy, only we who carry the obligation to sustain. Nature-inspired learning and leading instructs us to look, see, feel, and act upon the force for evil we impose, the risks we face, the means we have at our disposal to steward, and the compulsion we have to act.

I carry my obligation to the earth in my very blood. When we moved to Urbana, Ohio in 2008, our son-in-law—digging into his in-laws' genealogy—discovered that my paternal great, great, great, great, great grandfather is buried in Urbana. John Dawson fought in the American Revolution. We found his gravesite and its ornate tombstone intricately engraved with a massive oak tree with spreading crown depicted as the tree of life.

Grandpa John Dawson must have been a tree devotee, or perhaps saw some powerful totem in the oak. What meaning can I decipher from our moving to a place I never knew existed, only to find a notable ancestor buried just a mile and a half away, and then to find the magnificent tree-emblazoned tombstone? I'll accept it as too strong to be coincidence. Instead, I see it as a correspondence: an alignment of deeper essence, a symbol too meaningful to ignore. I'll embrace the message as a call that I am living a life directed by heritage, by a bloodline that orients me to trees—and through trees, to nature and to Earth.

I recognize that nature-inspired leading found me at the moment when Earth and our species need it most. Grandpa Dawson is speaking to me across the ages since his death well over 200 years ago. I cannot ignore the call to spread the gospel of Earth stewardship. Nature depends on us to practice the tenets of sustainability as we live, learn, serve, and lead.

Spirit and Matter: The Ultimate Unity

A Guest Essay by Ray Silverman

I first met Steve Jones when he was the president of Urbana University. At the time, I was doing research for a book on Johnny Appleseed, famous for distributing apple seeds, but little known as a distributer of spiritual truth. Wherever he went, Johnny distributed the teachings of Emanuel Swedenborg who once said, "The whole world of nature is a theatre representative of the invisible spiritual world (1978)."

Urbana University houses The Johnny Appleseed Museum— home of the largest collection of Johnny Appleseed memorabilia in the world. At the entrance to this historic museum is an apple tree, a direct descendent of one of Johnny's original saplings. Inside the building, amid numerous books, articles, and Appleseed artifacts, is a copy of Johnny's original Bible. In Johnny Appleseed, the world of nature (planting apple seeds) and the world of spirit (planting spiritual truth) were one.

During my weeklong stay at Urbana, it was my pleasure to be the guest of Steve and Judy Jones, who provided food and shelter during my research sojourn. Steve was not only a gracious host, but also an incisive reader of my budding manuscript. For example, he helped me differentiate between "seedlings" and "saplings," as well as between "nurseries" and "orchards." To me, untrained in horticulture, these terms seemed to be synonymous. But to someone who has been growing plants since childhood, and has a Ph.D. in forestry as well, these distinctions are significant.

When I completed my research, and readied the manuscript for publication, I concluded the acknowledgments section with the metaphor of "the swarm." The idea comes from *Ecological Intelligence* by Daniel Goleman, an audio book I had been listening to during my nine-hour drive to Urbana. In describing the mystery of the swarm, Dan refers to it as "collective distributed intelligence." I was so struck by this concept that I recorded a voice memo on my phone as I cruised along the interstate. I said:

> "*Collective Distributed Intelligence*. This is what we need in the twenty-first century, says Dan Goleman. I'm thinking of this in terms of the Johnny Appleseed book. I could never have done all of this by myself . . . so many people came together to help me bring to others *The Core of Johnny Appleseed*. In the coming age, the model is the swarm—a swarm of ants, a swarm of bees, a swarm of human beings, working together, sharing what they know, creating a better world and a brighter tomorrow."

This was the end of my "Acknowledgments" section. I then added, "And so, to the whole swarm who gathered to help produce this book, I say, with deepest gratitude, 'Thank you.'"

Similarly, as I conclude my brief contribution to this book of collected essays, I say, "Thank you for allowing me to be a member of your swarm." And thank you to the Invisible Leader of the Swarm, the One who mysteriously brings us all together, helping us to see spirit in terms of matter, and matter in terms of spirit.

Bio

Ray Silverman, Ph.D., serves as Associate Professor of English and Religion at Bryn Athyn College in Bryn Athyn, PA. He is the editor and reviser of Helen Keller's *Light in My Darkness,* the co-author of *Rise Above It: Spiritual Development through the Ten Commandments,* and the author of *The Core of Johnny Appleseed: The Unknown Story of a Spiritual Trailblazer.* He is a member of the University of Delaware Institute for Transforming Higher Education and a founding member of the Nature Based Leadership Institute.

Risk Mitigation and Value Creation

~ Nature has practiced the craft for eons ~

In the fall of 2014, Lina Constantinovici—San Francisco-based entrepreneur and one of the Nature Based Leadership Institute founders—invited me to present to a Bay Area conference the following April. The conference theme was "Risk and Value, Learning from 4.5 Billion Years of Life." I agreed to make a 15-minute presentation entitled: "Lessons from Nature in Risk Mitigation and Value Creation." But I had one caveat: I could not present in-person and would instead deliver via video. Lina and I were already scheming to create the entity that has since evolved into the Antioch University New England Nature Based Leadership Institute. April in San Francisco would be a trial balloon, testing whether this new notion of nature-inspired leadership might find traction.

I devoted a lot of thought to a crisp fifteen-minute introduction. I offer the text of my remarks below. Following the transcription, I provide reflections now a year and half beyond that presentation.

Well, Good Afternoon! I wish I could be there with you. However, as you hear my words, my wife and I will be in Washington D.C. with our seven-year-old grandson, on a trip we have long planned, his first away from his mom and dad.

I want to talk to you about lessons from nature involving risk management and value creation. This past winter—a very rough one here in New England—I spent hours watching microenterprises, a blur of action as they mitigated risk, created value, and dealt with competitors and predators, in effect avoiding death and starvation. In some ways it sounds like a typical day at the office.

Me? I'm a forester, a lifelong outdoorsman, a naturalist who just happens to be a university president. Now, 42 years beyond my undergraduate degree, I am ever more committed to the notion that every lesson for living, for learning, for managing, for leading is written indelibly, emphatically, repeatedly, and reliably in nature.

Let me give you an example of a powerful lesson I drew from nature. [Note: I included the following tale in "Nature Based Leadership." I repeat it in this second book because it never fails to carry an audience and I can think of nothing more critical to leadership than a dual shot of humility and inspiration. The combination is essential, and it is drawn nowhere better than from nature.] This happened while I was in Alaska serving as the chancellor at the University of Alaska Fairbanks. From our campus, many colleagues told me that on a very clear day we could actually see Denali: North America's highest mountain at 20,310 feet. However, in my first two months, Denali always stood shrouded in clouds. I had still not seen the mountain. We had scheduled an early September trip, driving the 90 miles to the entrance of Denali National Park. There we hopped aboard a friend's single engine Cessna, and flew the additional ninety miles back to Kantishna, a lodge, and a gravel landing strip about eighteen miles north of the mountain.

Cloudy all the way back, we could see only the lower third of Denali. And even in that one-third vertical exposure, we saw grandeur: magnificent glaciers, rock faces, snow fields. Clouds obscured everything above 7,000 feet. We landed at the gravel airstrip. From Kantishna, even if it had been clear, we wouldn't have seen Denali from the lodge. Thirty-five hundred foot Mt. Quigley stood to the south of Kantishna, blocking our view.

Next morning, we arose early to find the sky perfectly clear. However, we did not want to elevate our hope—the mountain often generates its own weather, enfolding its upper reaches in dense clouds. I decided to get out ahead of my colleagues, lacing my hiking boots, sipping the last of my coffee, and beginning the trek up Quigley.

The ascent went very smoothly, mostly along an old Jeep trail. I watched with great pride—I admit to even a sense of smugness—as the gravel Kantishna airstrip began to shrink while I ascended far above it. The flat plains to the north stretched endlessly to the horizon. And finally, near the top of Quigley, I was feeling full of myself. Man, I had *climbed* Quigley; the airstrip was barely visible in the valley below. I had left my companions far below, out of sight. The day was mine; I had secured some kind of yet-to-be-defined victory!

As the trail began to flatten, I paused. I had been watching my footfalls on the densely-cobbled surface; I didn't want to fall on my face. Pausing, I felt the presence of something. You know how you feel when you think somebody is watching or looking at you? I detected that kind of presence. And sensing that I was no longer alone, I directed my gaze to the south, where I knew Denali stood. I was unprepared. There before me was something unlike anything I had ever seen before. My eyes first looked horizontally... and then up, and up, and up, and up. There before me stood 18,000 vertical feet of snowfields, glaciers, rock faces. This gleaming, white magnificence stood in the morning sunlight. And in that instant I felt absolute humility! I had done nothing in climbing Quigley. In fact, everything I had done in my five-plus decades preceding that moment felt totally insignificant.

However, at that same moment of total humility, I felt infinite inspiration. Full humility and unsurpassed inspiration, absolute and overwhelming! The lesson that I want to convey to you from that experience is that we need—all of us—to employ humility and find inspiration in everything we do.

Shift gears now to a simple flower. The purpose of that flower is to attract pollinators, and produce viable seed. Louie Schwartzberg in *Nature, Beauty, and Gratitude* observed that beauty and seduction are nature's tools for survival. How does this relate to what you do in running your enterprises? Stop and think about any advertising media. It depends entirely on seduction and beauty.

Now, from the aromatic beauty of a rose to a much larger enterprise, an oak tree... It is massive, stationary, and long-lived. The oak tree seeks to flourish, to reproduce, to provide for future generations. The enterprise seeks to be the *mighty oak*. Henry Wadsworth Longfellow observed that the purpose of a tree is to grow a little new wood each year. And so it is with the oak.

But, there are risks. Like wind, a powerful risk factor. The tree has to produce, in risk mitigation, wood for the stem, for the branches, for the trunk, and for the roots, and to do so year after year after year. Another risk is competition from other plants. The mitigation strategy that the oak employs is to be ever growing, capturing more territory, accessing additional resources in the soil by extending the roots, and seeking more and more direct sunlight by extending its branches horizontally and vertically. The oak, like any enterprise, has only limited resources to allocate to the different parts of the tree. Does it allocate the resources to wood, roots, leaves: today's enterprise? Or to acorns that do nothing for the tree itself but extend the business forward? It's a constant balance in any enterprise between enriching today's operation, and investing in the future. The lesson is simple: any enterprise must allocate resources thoughtfully, deliberately, systematically, and in some kind of balance.

We can draw general, yet universal lessons from oaks: any enterprise is only as strong as its weakest link. Try being a mighty oak with a weak trunk. It can't be done. Location is also critical. Try being a mighty oak on an upper convex slope with shallow soils and a wind-swept position. It can't be done. Another important lesson is to develop reciprocal relationships. Think about the oak tree and the squirrel. The oak invests tremendous resources into producing an acorn crop. The squirrel is there ready to devour them. The squirrel is dependent on the oak. However, the oak often produces more acorns at any one time than the squirrel can consume, and the squirrel very smartly caches the acorns—buries them under the leaves and places them with the idea that she'll come back, find them, and eat them. But squirrels aren't smart enough to remember every acorn planted. For the tremendous price the oak tree pays in producing the acorn, the squirrel benefits and, in turn, pays a dividend forward by planting a few acorns she fails to recover. It's a reciprocal relationship.

Another lesson from the oak tree is to plan and prepare for adversity. Every winter, all the oak trees here in New England dutifully transition into dormancy in the late fall, preparing for six months of weather adversity. It works quite well. Withstanding bitter winter is one thing. Fire is yet another natural element of adversity. However, the mighty oak grows a thick, corky bark, and as the spring fire rushes through the stand, the bark is thick enough to keep the flames from doing any damage. The seedling is another story with respect to fire. The spring fire consumes the seedling above the ground line. The species knows the drill, having dealt with spring fires across the eons. Dormant buds on upper roots beneath the burn zone spring to life; a new oak seedling sprouts from the hidden and protected buds—a wonderful, time-tested risk mitigation.

I will read to you now a poem from one of my favorite authors: Robert Service, a Brit who lived in the great northwest Yukon of Canada at the turn of the prior century. Service wrote a lot of powerful poems. This one, from *The Collected Poems of Robert Service*, is called "Security." If I were there with you I would ask and look for a response, "Do any of you know what a limpet is?" But I can't see your response, so I will tell you. A limpet is a sea creature that is two to three inches tall. It grows in intertidal zones anchored firmly to the rocks. They are actually quite tasty raw, by the way.

[Note: At this point in my presentation I read "Security" in its entirety to the audience; it is about a foolish limpet who wants to be freed from her anchorage but ends up getting eaten by a crab. I continued with the following remarks.]

"Don't take the chance of the changing sea, But—cling like hell to your rock." The lesson is pretty simple: stick to your values, cling to your principles, hold to your beliefs. It's essential wisdom and guidance for any enterprise.

So, whether a sparrow, a mighty oak, a corner grocer, or a multinational corporation, the nature based enterprise tenets are the same:

- Choose the right location.
- Compete effectively.
- Watch for predators.
- Live long.
- Anticipate and prepare for adversity.
- Partner with others.
- Plan for succession into the future.
- Beware the siren song of beauty and seduction.
- Add a little new wood each year.
- Cling like hell to your rock.

So, nature's lessons for risk mitigation and value creation are tried and true. They're honed through the eons; they're shaped by evolution. Many, many more lessons I am certain await our discovery. What more *can* we learn? What more *should* we learn? All of us want to learn. We need to know what those lessons might be. We have only this one chance as business practitioners, as leaders, and as Earth stewards, to get it right.

Our obligation at Antioch University New England carries back to 1859 when our founding president Horace Mann said to the first graduating class, "Be ashamed to die until you have won some victory for humanity." It's part of our university DNA. Our *modus operandi* as an institution has roots that remain anchored in Mann's long-ago admonition and challenge; they carry the essence forward to today. Our MO is to help our students see issues in other dimensions, to see deeply enough to generate feelings—those of empathy, concern, sincerity—and to generate an obligation to address those issues. The imperative is to generate feelings deep enough to inspire and enable action. Unless we act, nothing changes. We have seen, felt, and are now taking action with respect to nature based leadership here at Antioch New England. We've recently created our Nature Based Leadership Institute.

I urge you to do the following.

Watch for more; keep track of us. We are taking shape, working closely with Lina and others right there on the west coast. We're identifying needs. We're seeking partners. And although I can't be there with you today, Don Woodhouse from Antioch University New England is there. Because I can't stand up there and wave my arms, I'm asking Don to please stand up, and wave your arms. I encourage and implore all of you to seek out Don and talk to him.

So I leave you with warm wishes for all that lies ahead beyond this conference, and I hope somehow we at Antioch New England can be part of your future. Thank you.

Comedian Tommy Smothers once said, "When you don't know what you're talking about, it's hard to know when you're finished." My video presentation preparation consumed many hours. I wanted to make sure I knew what I was talking about so I could bring the topic into crisp focus and firm closure. Crystalizing complex ideas into simple words can be extraordinarily exhausting, yet there is no other way to distill the essence of an idea into the seed from which a movement might germinate. I view nature-inspired learning and leading as a movement. Its lessons are so fundamental. Its illustrations—because they are rooted in the natural world with its richness and beauty—can be powerful far beyond the sterile case studies that otherwise portray leadership literature. Think about the simple lessons I presented to the San Francisco participants:

- Try leading without humility and inspiration. Quigley and Denali are wonderful metaphors.
- Beauty and seduction are powerful forces for good and evil. I used the simple flower, yet other examples from nature are endless. There is the seduction employed by the angler fish, presenting the lure from an appendage suspended in front of its massive jaws, or the sundew with its sweet nectar drawing insects into a terminally sticky trap of death.

- To succeed we must understand limitations and appreciate the factors of production. The mighty oak teaches us that even in nature location (and the relationships inherent in location) influences success and failure.
- No enterprise or individual exists without reciprocal relationships. No leader thrives without that understanding, just as the oak does not operate in isolation. The oak enjoys a magic reciprocity with the forest's arboreal rodents.
- Every enterprise must anticipate adversity and prepare for it; this is resilience.
- We need to balance immediate return with enterprise sustainability. Does the oak invest in the engine of today (leaves and related) or extend its reach into the next century and beyond, i.e. acorns?
- Ethics and values are paramount: "cling like hell to your rock."

The San Francisco venue provided a great opportunity for giving definition to the nature based leadership concept. The nearly-two years that stand between that first attempt to shape the concept succinctly and to test whether or not others found traction in it shows that they did. Granted, the *movement* remains a hope, even as the idea seems to generate lots of interest and enthusiasm. I am ever more convinced that we have identified a vacuum and a deep need. I see an imperative for an expanding human recognition that nature can furnish many of the ideas and provide much of the inspiration for society to recognize, understand, and act on *Caring for Our Common Home*, the title of Pope Francis' 2015 Encyclical. The time is now, before we as a species pass a threshold, to embrace an Earth ethic and practice responsible Earth stewardship. Nature-inspired learning and leading offers the lessons, inspires the obligation, and enables the action.

Because I am a forester with deep and abiding passion for trees and forests, I will not resist expanding the oak tree's nature-inspired lessons much more deeply. I envision another essay devoted to the mighty oak in my third book.

Pressures and Thresholds

~ Like most forces of nature: living, learning, serving, and leading are incremental ~

Equilibrium is a state in which opposing forces or influences are balanced. We all strive for such equilibrium in our lives. Nature seeks it as well, achieving balance occasionally with smooth ease. Morning sun warms the coastal plains much more rapidly than it affects the ocean surface. Air warmed over the land lifts (basic laws of atmospheric physics, buoyancy, and lapse rates), generating a sea breeze as the denser, cooler ocean air sweeps in to replace the rising air. Those mornings of gradual warming, lifting, and replacement witness a smooth equilibrating. Yet, under the right conditions—a saturated and unstable air mass with a steeply negative vertical temperature profile, for example—the morning sea breeze front can kick off a line of thundershowers moving inland. Such was the case many mid- and late-summer mornings when I lived in Savannah, GA. The right conditions, along with a trigger, shift the transition from smooth to heavy downpours, although seldom did these showers generate damaging winds.

The Mississippi River swells annually with spring rains and up-basin snowmelt. Old Muddy carries a dense sediment load, and has for time immemorial. Before the Army Corps of Engineers levy construction, the river annually escaped its channel, overflowed its banks, and deposited a sediment layer on thousands of square miles of delta, including the greater New Orleans region. The deposits in some places reach tens of thousands of feet thick, heavy enough to subside the crustal plate at a pace roughly in equilibrium with the annual sediment deposit. Prior to the levy system, the delta appeared to be static, neither rising nor falling. Thanks to the unintended consequence of channeling annual floods south to the Gulf of Mexico, the delta and New Orleans continued to subside, now without annual deposition. Nature's smooth balance assured equilibrium. Today, parts of New Orleans are ten feet below sea level. Another Katrina is inevitable. The next one may not be so kind. Nature offers to teach us yet we turn a blind eye, thinking we are in control. John McPhee, in *The Control of Nature*, observed of the economic forces at play,

> "The industries were there because of the river. They had come for its navigational convenience and its fresh water. They would not, and could not, linger beside a tidal creek. For nature to take its course was simply unthinkable. The Sixth World War would do less damage to southern Louisiana. Nature, in this place, had become an enemy of the state."

Antioch University New England's 2016 student commencement speaker, Dr. Jason Rhoades (hooded at the ceremony after speaking), communicated lessons and wisdom from nature:

> "We might consider the outcome of a single initiative relative to its intended outcome as an indication of success or failure. I propose that we think along the lines of the movement of tectonic plates: slow incremental movements over sometimes-great periods of time, building of pressure, grinding away. And then in an instant you have an earthquake. Now it would be foolish to label the intervening building of pressure "a failure." And it would be equally foolish to highlight the moment of the earthquake "a success." The

earthquake would simply not exist without prolonged effort and adaptability and resilience through that long time when outwardly little [is] evident."

Jason nailed it. Much of our work remains hidden from results until we reach an inflection point, and cumulative trigger. Nature tells us that cumulative effect over time yields results. Nature speaks clearly about what appears to be at equilibrium masking tremendous forces that are, for the moment, balanced; yet in another moment there is violent release, or a cataclysm. I write these words one day after the 36th anniversary of the eruption of Mount St. Helens. Then and now St. Helens is a majestic Cascade Mountains peak, appearing to the unknowing eye as serene and peaceful. Yet seismologists and volcanologists in the spring of 1980 monitored its bulging north flank and very active magma core with alarm (and professional captivation). One moment, powerful forces were at equilibrium; the next, the north flank fractured, the mountainside collapsed to the north, and spectacular energy explosively blasted outward and upward.

But I am not promoting violent release and cataclysmic results for our daily activities. I offer a more benign example from nature.

Our daily walk where we lived in New Hampshire took us along a country lane bordered by fencerow sugar maples, oak, hickories, white pine, and an occasional black cherry. Some reach a 30-inch diameter at breast height. We thrilled at the woodpecker evidence and sometimes the birds in action as they worked the dead and dying snags among the probably 150-year-old sentries. For three years, we walked the route and paid special attention to a long-dead snag (a maple I believe, but bark long shed and wood badly decaying) approaching three feet in diameter and still 30 feet tall. We wondered how long it would remain vertical. An early April morning after a wet and windy night we had our answer. The spongy decayed wood had absorbed a heavy load of rain, the wind gave one last push, and equilibrium yielded to gravity. The fallen log entered a new stage in the life of the road/wood edge ecosystem, still adding value and serving a higher purpose.

Living, learning, serving, and leading are incremental, just like the forces of nature. The final blow of the axe brings the tree to the ground, yet every single strike contributes equally. So it goes with our work, our service, and our families. Every action is a force applied to the aggregate. Progress may be apparent inch by inch. Often it occurs in jumps and starts as we pass critical thresholds. Still, it is the relentless application of time, wisdom, energy, action, and passion that triggers the movement and yields results.

Depending upon purpose and desired outcome, the result can be viewed as positive or negative. Mount St. Helens offered no opinion on the events of May 18, 1980. The life of a volcano just is. Our earth is dynamic, ever changing, with powerful forces in constant flux. However, that volcanic day saw lives lost, homes destroyed, forests leveled, businesses terminated, and a region altered for centuries. The mountain just did what active volcanoes do. It is we who must understand, anticipate, and recover from the ways of nature.

Forests immediately north of St. Helens are healing. Once more trees reach for sunlight, streams run clear, the trout have returned. Wildlife is once more abundant; beauty and serenity are ubiquitous. The mountain does not notice. Occasional grunts and burps and steam and smoke contradict the seeming docile wonder and magic. The forces will once more edge past a critical threshold; that's what active volcanoes do. Because nature actually does abhor a vacuum, the forest will again reclaim a seemingly devastated landscape.

Consider, too, the Yellowstone caldera, perhaps the world's largest geologically-active hot spot. Old Faithful, hot springs, and a bulging caldera surface signal that many miles below the earth's surface there is unrest. Within the enterprise in which you devote your heart, passion, knowledge, and work, what does the superficial evidence foretell? Are you watching, monitoring, and anticipating? Or are you blind to the pressures building? I urge you, as does the wisdom of nature, to look deeply and with understanding.

I heard of a university that suffered prolonged operating stress: weakening market position, persistent administrative and leadership failings, an apparent inability or unwillingness to change direction, faculty frustration and dismay, and flagging enrollment. These are the aggregate tectonic forces for institutional demise. Without radical intervention and a leadership transfusion, eventually the plates leap, the Richter needle dances wildly, and a resultant quake shakes the university into oblivion. A sort of *natural* death. Adept leadership would have noticed the metaphoric north flank bulging, anticipated catastrophic consequences, and taken emergency corrective actions. Such jeopardy is the case with any enterprise that is blind to the forces affecting it.

Nature instructs us to look for signs and signals. It teaches us to interpret their meanings. Nature counsels us to mitigate, resist, and act in anticipation. Too many people are simply blind, unwilling, or unable to look and see. Too often the consequences of inaction are fatal to the enterprise. Nature usually offers warning to those who know to look and have the tools and wisdom to see. Nature's signals are easy to interpret, easy for those who can translate the language. Enterprise health metrics are likewise at hand, and translatable for those who care to monitor and who are prepared to act.

We humans are adding pressures to the intricate web of life and interactions that sustain us. Do we fully comprehend the checks and balances we are affecting? Can we anticipate when the metaphorical crustal plates can no longer hold? When the thresholds might be surpassed? When the north flank will give way? When atmospheric greenhouse gases will reach a climate tipping point? When population and consumption will exceed Earth's carrying capacity? Are we heeding Pope Francis' plea to care for our home?

We cannot prevent the Yellowstone caldera from one day releasing the unfathomable pressure building deep below the surface of that globally significant landscape, itself created from a previous blast. We cannot prevent the San Andreas Fault from once again surpassing a tensile point of release. We certainly cannot stop Old Muddy from once again breaching the levees—perhaps with the help of the next Katrina—that merely delay nature's ultimate victory over our feeble attempts to control it. I am not one to cry despair or to preach gloom and doom. Instead, I beseech us to understand the perils. If we live near the fault, anticipate the power of the release that is inevitable and will likely occur within our lifetime. If we visit Yellowstone, be aware of the force that created it, and appreciate that those forces remain in place; all the while be mindful that a repeat performance—while perhaps inevitable—is not imminent and could lie tens of thousands of years into a distant future. Have faith that the Yellowstone caldera will send us signals of cataclysm in time to escape its reach. The next Katrina will not give years or even weeks' notice. We can plan only for timely and efficient evacuation.

By and large, these pressures are natural. Their consequences impact us only to the extent we build, live, work, and play within the respective impact zones. One could not pay me enough to live or work on the subsiding delta in New Orleans at ten feet (and counting) below sea level. I will still visit (but not during the humidity and heat blasts of summer). I will happily sit below sea level at Café Du Monde enjoying sinfully decadent beignets on a delightful spring morning. Likewise, I'll risk a trip to San Francisco every 3-5 years for a shrimp salad on sourdough at Fisherman's Warf. And this coming summer I will visit the Greater Yellowstone ecosystem at Teton Science Schools.

Among the three destinations, only one gives me any pause, and even that one is not enough to dissuade me. EarthquakeSafety.com indicates:

> "California has more than a 99% chance of having a magnitude 6.7 or larger earthquake within the next 30 years, according to scientists using a new model to determine the probability of big quakes."

And the San Andreas stretches for 800 miles. I think the chances are pretty good that I can whisk in to the Bay Area, enjoy that sandwich, grab a bite in Chinatown, spend a couple of nights, and depart before the walls come tumbling down. I'll simply watch for tropical systems in the Gulf of Mexico before flying in for a beignet. As for fear of the caldera blowing, driving any road in America is far more dangerous and risky.

However, what notice will we get to prepare and act in response to the other kinds of human-influence overloading we might trigger? Do we know the thresholds? Can we anticipate results? Are we looking, seeing, feeling, and acting at sufficient resolution? Nature-inspired learning and leading instructs us to examine those unknowns, and reminds us that we rely upon this earth to sustain us. We cannot sit blissfully in our protected cocoons thinking that we are somehow separate from the environment. Instead, we are one with the world within which we live, and upon which we are absolutely, completely, and inextricably dependent. As Carl Sagan reminded us 30 years ago, we reside on a pale blue orb, a mote of dust in the vast darkness of space. What will it take to awaken us to the realities of that relationship and the frailties of our utter dependence? Nature-inspired learning and leading is not intended to frighten us into action. Instead, I believe it awakens us to our need to soberly recognize and confront the true picture.

As with living, learning, serving, and leading, we must know the terrain, understand the risks and exposure, and make informed decisions. And yet societally, we seem blind to conditions we are creating on our small world, and the pressures we are imposing. We seem to not comprehend the potential cataclysmic failure that could result. What if the National Science Foundation issued the following statement: "human society has more than a 99 percent chance of exceeding Earth's sustainable carrying capacity within the next 30 years, according to scientists using a new model to determine the probability that we are self-destructing"?

Nature-inspired learning and leading will not save us from ourselves. In fact, nature's wisdom will not raise issues new to us, nor shout alarms previously uncried. What we hope to do is apply a different lens, employ a different megaphone. We aren't planning to find every answer. Instead, we hope to lead more individuals, communities, businesses, and organizations to find the right questions. We note that many people—especially those who are apt to hear and then heed our message—do pay attention to nature. Carl Sagan said we are alone in the vast darkness of space; no one will come from somewhere else to save us. In the absence of such a rescue ship, we want to awaken our collective conscience before the hourglass empties. We will only have this one chance to get it right.

Robert Frost revealed clear wisdom in "The Road Not Taken." We all know the words and their deep meaning. He saw the obvious result of so many of our life's choices; we move beyond that decision in a manner that does not swing back around. In the spirit of Frost's prophetic insight, perhaps we who are founding this emerging nature-inspired learning and leading movement somewhat conceitedly see our approach to encouraging Earth stewardship as new, fresh, and groundbreaking—the road not taken. We imagine that we are embarking on a road not just less traveled, but perhaps one previously untrodden at all. Jared Diamond (in *Collapse, How Societies Choose to Fail or Succeed*) believes that prior human societies made fatal blind decisions that brought an end to otherwise-flourishing societies. However, right now appears to be the first time that we have brought a so-called intelligent global society to the brink. Nature's wisdom will prompt the right questions, seek engagement to refine the message and spread the gospel, as well as offer a new approach to helping people look, see, feel, and act. We must get it right!

Ironically, I am making edits to this manuscript late in August 2016, just eight weeks since Antioch University leadership elected to consolidate the five-campus system resulting in my current state as "past president." I now stand metaphorically where several roads diverge in a yellow wood. Perhaps I should seek guidance from nature, which only seems appropriate for the person who helped develop the concept of the term nature based leadership. I believe I am still adding new wood each year. April's soaking rains and fresh breezes do not yet threaten to place me horizontal, and recycle me as forest floor duff. I have value yet to give toward ensuring a brighter tomorrow. I will postpone retirement! I pledge to accelerate and amplify championing the cause of nature-inspired learning and leading.

Seeing What Lies Hidden Within

~ Opening our eyes to the unseen
in nature and in life ~

Consider the Himalayas, rising nearly five miles above sea level. Their angular spires would stand even higher were it not for the scouring force derived from time, gravity, and ice. Mountains despise glaciers, yet it is mountains that create their chief antagonists. Those very highlands wring heavy snows from air masses and storms rushing over the heights. Across a vast zone of the Himalayan plateau's upper reaches, low temperatures sustain the snowpack year-round. This is the zone of accumulation, the glacier-birthing region. Time increases the snow, each season adding and compressing deeper and deeper. Gravity and physics transform the fluffy white powder to glacial ice. As the ice thickens, it assumes a greater plasticity, beginning to accept the forces of gravity to flow downhill.

Nothing in nature is static. For every action, there is an equal and opposite reaction. Great weight and gravity's draw find release in horizontal force, exerting the ice to find exits downhill, hence the *rivers* of ice. Just as the snowfields gleam their brilliant and pristine white, so, too, do the outlets. Still, the appearance from an aircraft suggests calmness and serenity, a seeming static beauty. A splendor that belies what lies within, hidden to all but those who discern and interpret her signals.

I flew low over vast snowfields high in the Alaska Range and over the Wrangell Saint Elias Mountains in Southeast Alaska. Pure white, hemmed by spectacular peaks, the snowfields did not hint at the power they furnish to the majestic rivers of ice that drain from them. Where the rivers drop over ledges and the pitch steepens, ice falls—jumbles of massive, cracked and fissured ice blocks, and silent crevasses—hint that the flow is not smooth, gentle, nor laminar. Unlike liquid whitewater, the pace does not appear violent and turbulent. Yet it clearly is, though muted and softened, its movement invisible with a single glance. In fact, we are blind to its slow motion, mountain-busting violence. What we cannot detect scars the mountain, inexorably and indelibly. Snow carpets the winter valley with a gentle, loving kiss, while at higher elevation it delivers the black widow's terminal caress. Ultimately, the mountain will succumb to its lover's will, to her ceaseless embrace.

Once below the zone of accumulation and into the region of ablation (where summer's melting exceeds annual snowfall), the glacier begins to signal more clearly what it has wrought on its journey. Above the ablation zone, the glacier hides its labor and toil under permanent snow cover as well as beneath its flowing ice. Summers in the ablation zone peel away the mask of stillness. Striations of dark debris—rocks, dirt, and boulders—parallel the direction of flow, signaling the power and brute force of massive ice scraping the reluctantly yielding bedrock. Lateral moraines border the ice along valley walls. If the glacier gives way to ultimate melting on land, terminal moraines tower at the end point. Where the ice-river ends in a marine environment, the terminal moraine resides subsurface, still hidden.

Surging summer meltwater at the terminus also evidences the glacier's power. Heavily silt-laden, the meltwater carries a tremendous load of rock-flour scoured by the grinding ice. Near Fairbanks where the clear Chena River enters the Tanana, glacier-fed from the Alaska Range, the contrast is stark. The roiling clouds of the Tanana's milky water intermingle turbulently with the Chena's clear input. Downstream, the two become homogenous, still appearing heavily silt-bearing owing to the far greater volume of the Tanana.

Now, picture the Appalachians—*ancient* alpine remnants long since water-worn, softened by time. Their valleys are V-shaped, a signature of water-wear. Shifting to New Hampshire's White Mountains, with U-shaped valleys, cols, and cirques, features bear witness to their somewhat *recent* glaciation (12 thousand years ago).

Everywhere, it is the land itself that demonstrates the power of flowing ice. Glaciers, borne of the mountains, simply do as they are designed: find outlet to lower elevations. There is no judgment of glaciers and mountains; one is as good as the other. Both offer us short-lived humans the gift of unmatched beauty and deep inspiration. Their continuous coexistence yields metaphorical wisdom.

All of us engage in such ceaseless interaction, often invisible to others as they are hidden beneath veneers of our own design. We feel the relentless power of external forces—scouring and wearing—shaping our mind, heart, body, spirit, and soul. We choose as individuals whether the sculpting works wonder and magic, or exacts the scars of pain, anger, pride, and judgment. We, like mountains, must ultimately wash to the sea. Life for humans and for mountains is finite. We can hope only to do our small part to ensure that the land and we (as a species) persevere across the sweep of time. Louis Bromfield captured that personal obligation perfectly in *Pleasant Valley*, his book-length tale of reclaiming the health and vitality of Malabar Farm, the "worn out," north-central Ohio property he bought in 1939.

> "The adventure at Malabar is by no means finished… The land came to us out of eternity and when the youngest of us associated with it dies, it will still be here. The best we can hope to do is to leave the mark of our fleeting existence upon it, to die knowing that we have changed a small corner of this earth for the better by wisdom, knowledge, and hard work."

John McPhee noted in *Basin and Range*,

> "If by some fiat I had to restrict all this writing to one sentence, this is the one I would choose: The summit of Mt. Everest is marine limestone."

That single statement symbolizes the endless cycles of life and living, sustaining across the eons. Everest's peak is calcareous rock seeded long ago in a warm, shallow sea of debris, in part washed from ancient mountains long since eroded by agents of relentless destruction. Mountains despise glaciers, yet the meltwater carries sediment that will rise again.

Today, somewhere in a warm shallow sea, a future Mount Everest lies in wait, likewise hidden from view. The young couple snorkeling in those placid waters sees no evidence of what lies ahead, or of what came before. We are creatures of the moment, blind to all that we cannot or refuse to see. Much in nature that is powerful and destructive lies shrouded by overwhelming beauty and unmatched inspiration. Consider a super-cell thunderstorm, one dropping an EF-5 tornado, viewed from 50 miles away across the verdant spring plains of Oklahoma: a magnificent, gleaming, towering cumulonimbus, not the terror at ground level a mile in front of the approaching growling, howling monster. Look at a satellite photo of Katrina mid-Gulf as she churned northward, a spectacularly menacing category-five hurricane, seeming docile, serene, and captivating from Earth orbit.

Few things in nature, business, and life reveal superficially what lies hidden within. It's only by learning the signs and signals that we can truly read beyond the cover. Importantly, nature does not choose to mask only its destructive forces. Virtually nothing is as it appears at first glance, or in the absence of prior experience, acquired familiarity, and learning. I can now *see* so much more, first because I choose to look in ways that that were beyond my reach and understanding in younger years. More is evident to me now because I recognize what I have seen and retain what I earlier learned. The image, the extraordinary lessons once learned, are indelible. Nature has told most of its stories many times before; over a lifetime, the retellings simply corroborate lessons already imprinted and internalized.

Whether we are interpreting the snowfield's pure white mask or a company's website green-washing, we must equip ourselves through experience and learning. We would do well to use the tools of discernment, the gifts of observation; we need to pay attention, draw conclusions, and be aware of our own exposure. And, we ought to be wary of the consequences of *not* looking, seeing, and understanding. Recall the sirens' song luring sailors to the rocky shoals and certain death.

We've known through history and ages of retold tales that beauty is only skin deep, that we should always look a gift horse in the mouth, and that you can't judge a book by its cover. The list is long, including this harsh Biblical wisdom in Matthew 23:27:

> "Woe to you, scribes and Pharisees, hypocrites! For you are like whitewashed tombs, which outwardly appear beautiful, but within are full of dead people's bones and pall uncleanness."

The grass is seldom greener on the other side of the fence.

So, what lies hidden within us? What shapes our own valleys? How have life and living sculpted us? How well can you read the superficial signs and signals of nature? What can you discern from outward appearances? Do you truly *see* what lies hidden within yourself, within nature, within others, within entities in your life? And, are you looking? Woe to those who do not look and at least attempt to see. We place ourselves at peril when we do not see beyond the mask of pure white, when we hear only the enchanted music of the sirens, when we inhale only the sweet magic of the sundew's nectar. What does our individual zone of ablation reveal? Are we making a difference? Are we shaping the world with positive intent? Are we winning victories for humanity?

What lessons lie hidden in nature? What are we learning from nature? We are asking these and many more questions through nature based leadership. We are encouraging, inspiring, and enabling leaders to *actually* look: to see purposely and thoughtfully, to see deeply enough to evoke feelings that discern right from wrong and sustainable from short term. We encourage activities that elicit feelings strong enough to spur action. For it is only via looking, seeing, feeling, and acting that we can sustain ourselves and win victories for humanity and nature. Nature-inspired learning and leading compels us to look within, even as we guide living, learning, serving, and leading in a manner that stewards our earth.

Only by seeing the invisible can we dream of doing the impossible in service to ourselves, the enterprises we lead, our communities, society, nations, and the planet. Far too many citizens and leaders are blind to what lies in front of them. Our blindness places us at peril. Our goal is to awaken the sense of sight, ignite commitment to action, and enable people to do what is right and sustainable. The time for applying nature's wisdom is now, before it is too late to rescue us from our blindness and ignorance.

"Vision is the art of seeing what is invisible to others."
Jonathon Swift

"My destination is no longer a place, rather a new way of seeing."
Marcel Proust

Inspired Pedaling

~ Nature's night illuminates
vision and opens eyes ~

My nature-inspired learning and leading journey interweaves through life, career, and recreational pursuits. Nature touches and defines so much of who I am. I offer a few paragraphs introduction to a memorable overnight experience that ties nature, service, and living to leading.

I served five years as president of Urbana University. In April each year our students, staff, and faculty would organize a community Relay for Life event to raise money for the fight against cancer. Beginning Friday afternoon, the event included games, music, and refreshments as individuals and teams walked loops through the night raising money from per-mile pledges.

That first year my early-to-bed-early-to-rise life pattern lengthened my night considerably. I enjoyed walking, talking, and cheering our participants. Yet the one-half-mile loop around (and around and around...) Urbana University's (frankly) rather uninspiring quad prompted me to consider how the next year I might suggest another element, one that would supplement the on-campus element, offer more challenge and inspiration during the night, and increase our financial support of the war against cancer.

As I describe more fully in my essay from the third year, we instituted an all-night biking alternative. Below I offer my Urbana University newsletter reflections from our inaugural 2010 biking component. I'll follow by more directly linking the experience to nature-inspired learning and leading.

We broke new ground Friday and Saturday April 16 and 17 in the Urbana University Relay for Life fight against cancer. You helped make it possible and I thank you! For those of you who pledged and donated, thank you for joining the fight. Some of you directed a portion of your donation to our Urbana University "wellness" program; we want to ensure that our employees and students recognize the importance of prevention and physical fitness in a life well-lived. For those who sponsored the ride, thank you for enabling a successful effort; we will prepare a letter for tax purposes formally acknowledging your in-kind or cash contribution.

To those who rode with me over segments of the 18 hours, please accept my heartfelt appreciation for making the long night manageable and enjoyable! I value all of you and dedicate my memories of the sojourn to you. Here is a reflective piece on the journey—a literal and figurative passage through time and geography. I'll begin with the end: 151 miles yielded a preliminary tally of raised dollars of $2,146 for the American Cancer Society, and $350 for our Urbana University wellness program.

I spent a total of 12 hours and 46 minutes actually in the saddle. As the night wore on, the stretching, eating, adding clothing, and recovery stops grew a little longer. Next year I'll strive for more pedal time! I owe a great deal to the riders who accompanied me from time to time: Cary Keller, Jacob Daniel, Christina DiGangi, Beth Paul, John Shingler, Nick Guidera, Bill Gregory, Megan Moser, Wendy Cromer, and—for his parallel riding in Florida—Noble Hendrix, who joined me by phone as he and his wife Patty, a cancer survivor, rode from six to eight PM.

Those with me at the onset "enjoyed" two brief thunderstorms, both with blasting wind, heavy rain, and face-stinging hail! A cold front provided the entertainment and ushered in the drier system that gave us the inspiring starlit night. The weather served as metaphor for our fight against cancer. We face in the disease a relentless storm; we seek a calm and starry sky, and the promise of a new day dawning. We began and ended the ride in sequence: we fought the elements, endured the darkness, and we greeted the new day crisp and clear with hope, promise, and delivery.

I want to offer a special thank you to Dr. Cary Keller, my dear friend from Fairbanks, Alaska, who traveled in excess of 4,000 miles to dedicate more than six hours and 80 miles to this effort. He offered an initial segment giving me comfort, company, and motivation through the storms and rejoined me for the last four hours as night gave way to first light. Making Cary's effort even more impressive is that the long Fairbanks winter allowed him only two training rides in preparation.

Another special note of appreciation goes to Wendy Cromer, UU volleyball coach, who accompanied me for 46 middle-of-the-night miles. Student Megan Moser rode ten of those wee hour miles with us; many thanks to Wendy and Megan for limiting my "alone" time to just two ten-mile loops the entire 18 hours. I offer a very special thank you to Beth Paul, who inspired all of us as she boldly tackled the storm alone after losing contact with us during the gale and hail. Because I don't want to risk leaving any rider out of the tale, please know that I am indebted to each of you who gave some of yourself to the cause and in support of my effort on the trail. Perhaps next year we can make the ride a formal and more encompassing part of the relay.

The ride serves as a metaphor for much of what we face at work, with family, and in many other elements of living. Life's circumstances require preparation; I forced myself to do many training rides during the brief springtime, totaling 370 miles. I envisioned the long night and prepared mentally for persevering and enduring. I thought many hours about the deep meaning and compelling cause of beating cancer; I knew that I would be part of a team effort and that many would depend upon me to maximize the per-mile pledges. I hoped to inspire others by giving this cause all I could and setting the dedication standard for others in years to come. And I rallied knowing that I would be serving a higher purpose and greater calling. We can't handle life's challenges unless we prepare: physically, mentally, emotionally, and spiritually. We need to maintain all four dimensions of fitness to ensure a life well-lived.

Each ten-mile loop I eagerly looked forward to two points. Halfway marked the first point of note; here we reversed direction in a trail parking area near Cedar Bog and dismounted for a swig of rehydration. During the long night we gasped in awe each time we saw the endless field of stars; we'd gaze deep into space through a long ago time and remember how small and insignificant we are, yet with purpose and meaning here in our earthly domain. The brief stop provided far more than hydration and a pause; it proved to be soul-nurturing in ways that none of us anticipated. The second beckoning point arrived at loop's end at the student center where we took an extended break, ate, drank, rested. Here we also had a chance to see the ground troops walking and walking and walking, relentlessly fighting the good fight and thereby giving the riders a dose of further inspiration.

Even as I relished the time with friends along the route, I cherished the two loops as a solitary rider through the night. We can never be all we might without time alone to reflect, digest, and think carefully.

I reflected on the B-25 formations with P-51 escorts that passed overhead repeatedly during the morning Friday. My dad, deceased for more than a decade, served the Pacific theater as Army Air Corps ground support during WWII. He loved airplanes, especially WWII vintage. We spread his ashes from a small plane over the grass airstrip where he would watch the action for hours at a time throughout his adult years. As I remembered him during Friday's WWII flights, tears of memory, joy, and sorrow blurred my vision, even as it inspired my purpose and commitment.

Symbolically, the 18-hour journey could not have ended better. Dr. Keller and I headed north to the airport as the B-25s lifted southbound for the day's activities at Wright Patterson; one after another they roared to life, headed down the runway, and lifted heavily into the air as we watched from our position just off the south end of the strip. Cary observed that each one provided an equal measure of awe, amazement, thrill, and inspiration. That is a perfect metaphor for life: the passage of one event or challenge should not dim our appreciation of the next. Friday night dished out a huge measure of inspiration and generated a full palette of possibilities. All of us at next year's relay will stand ready to roar and accelerate down the runway, lift into a sparkling clear sky, and make our way to another 18 hours of inspired purpose and action. So should it be with each challenge and opportunity along life's journey.

Thank you again for enabling a rewarding mission and successful flight!

Now six years after that inaugural journey, I extract some learned and earned lessons of nature-inspired learning and leading drawn from and inspired by that exquisite night. I'll begin with what at first will seem a non sequitur. Antioch University New England has a sister campus in Los Angeles. My counterpart there often chides me about our New Hampshire weather, particularly during extended winters. I acknowledge his kidding, telling him how fortunate he is to have such continuously perfect conditions all year long. Inside I am smiling; I utterly love the temperate climate extremes we enjoy here and in Ohio.

Throw me into the briar patch of wild frontal passages and the kind of major shifts we experienced during our April overnight ride! Nature's extremes serve as a defibrillator to recharge my heart and fuel my spirit and soul. I particularly thrill at being exposed in weather that approaches the scale of pleasurable terror! The two thunder showers that ushered the cold front through Ohio that spring evening came close. Watching such a squaw through a bay window supports the notion that so many people unfortunately "understand," that we are apart from nature. Sitting high on my road bike saddle pedaling into the teeth of the storm, lightning flashing, I was one with nature.

Nature-inspired learning and leading is rooted in appreciating that our brick, wood, and plaster-encased lives are inextricably tied to our intimate relationship with nature and this one earth with its finite resources. How can we possibly lead any enterprise from an ignorant and arrogant assumption that we operate apart from that natural world? There is no more palpable and powerful reminder of our total dependence upon nature than personally being exposed to the fury, beauty, awe, and wonder of it. There is no better way to appreciate our vulnerability than to be literally *one* with nature's magic. Had I been among those back on the quad walking the relay, I would have watched the brief fury from the student center lobby. Such a view is only weakly stimulating and far removed from the reality of humanity's relationship to nature. Nature-inspired learning and leading is about acknowledging that essential relationship between society and our environment—locally and globally, individually and collectively.

Biking through the hail and gale is total immersion, an education by trial. From the high saddle of a road bike, one can't help but look, see, feel, and act as one with nature. All who rode with me through the two storms felt the power, sensed the thrill, and marveled at what we had just experienced. They drew their own lessons from the pleasurable terror. From the student center lobby, they would have noticed the wind and rain, perhaps seen a small hail stone bounce on the lawn, and awaited the sun's return. Instead, we awaited calmer winds, clearing sky, and drying clothes. We reveled in nature's brief fury, and will always carry the memory of shared experience. Nature based leadership is helping fellow travelers appreciate and draw lessons from that common exposure. I pedaled and used the teachable moment to encourage others to see the invisible in those few minutes of wild weather.

How many other experiences in living, learning, serving, and leading unfold sequentially through uncertainty, peril, and darkness, followed by crisp dawning? Those 18 hours served as a metaphor for elements of any life worth living: challenge, durability, endurance, inspiration, humility, rest, renewal, hope, commitment, disappointments, satisfaction, and reward. The ride wove a spiritual thread, part of the fabric of my leadership garments. I find meaning and merit from such experiences that apply deeply to all that I do and that protect me from any elements of strife and turmoil I might yet encounter.

Life is a cycle of preparation, commitment, and action repeated time and time again as one journey leads to another, each intended to serve a higher purpose and greater calling. I contend that only nature can purely test our fitness for life. We lose sight of the ultimate purpose if we forget that all is embedded in our relationship to Earth. We cannot afford to live blindly and mutely under our well-insulated roof. Our relationship with Earth is absolute; we are fully dependent upon it.

Our human place in the cosmos lies in the vast, incomprehensible sweep of time. We are nothing, and yet we are everything. It's true in business, family, communities, and any enterprise. Earth resides on an arm of our rather insignificant Milky Way, one of two trillion such masses of stars. To reach the center of our galaxy a traveler would need 25,000 years moving at the speed of light: 186,000 miles per second. We are disconsolately alone. A starlit night on the bike is just one way to remind us that we live on a lifeboat in the vast darkness of space. Nature-inspired learning and leading demands that we recognize the irreconcilable burden of stewardship we bear.

I rejoiced recently in finding a relevant Ralph Waldo Emerson quote:

"Enthusiasm is the mother of effort, and without it nothing great was ever achieved."

At first glance, I thought, "Well, there you go: physical effort (like an all-night bike ride and the preparation for it) spurs and stimulates enthusiasm." But as I reread his words I realized that Emerson believes that enthusiasm *fuels* effort. I take issue with the one being independent of the other; I find enthusiasm and effort inseparable and absolutely interdependent. The combustion engine draws power from both fuel and oxygen. Spark it and we harness horsepower to do real work. I view enthusiasm and effort as synergistic elements of the power equation for living, learning, serving, and leading. Perhaps the necessary catalyst (the spark) is our individual will. It's a continuous, self-perpetuating loop. I'll accept this revelation as nature-inspired. And it's a lesson broadly applicable. We can do little without will, effort, and enthusiasm. Nature-inspired learning and leading suggests that we find all three ingredients in everything that we do.

Another lesson from that 18-hour stretch through time and geography is that quiet reflection and contemplation can be priceless. During my own marathon and distance running era, technology had introduced lightweight, high fidelity, battery-operated music devices to the fore. So many of my running contemporaries adopted the practice of running to their favorite tunes. I tried it and immediately abandoned the technology. How could I possibly improve upon shoulder season goose music, spring peepers, or pre-dawn bird calls? I opt for nature's musical accompaniment. And the introvert that I am relishes alone time. What better place than in nature to be solo; it's the only place where I find total solace! We cannot be truly effective in a world of twenty-four-hour distraction.

In sum, nature-inspired learning and leading taps the personal reservoir of lessons and inspiration garnered from experience in nature. Nothing activates our receptivity more effectively than a long night on the trail.

Kindred Spirits

A Guest Essay by Cary S. Keller

Steve Jones and I are kindred spirits. We are drawn outdoors to explore nature—humbled by its expanse, while eager to challenge its boundaries. We yearn for the personal growth that comes from immersion in nature. We relish the inspiration and insight that nature brings to solving and enjoying life challenges, as exemplified in the following three anecdotes.

I was backpacking through the Arctic tundra along the Kongakut River. Alone under the midnight sun, I hiked a narrow valley with steep sides. I felt a strange, distant percussion vibrate through me. It intensified progressively, an ominous feeling within me. Then I saw them: thousands of caribou filling the valley, thundering toward me. I was alarmed by the power of the herd and overwhelmed by the absence of any escape. I prepared to be trampled. I stood tall and faced the herd, making myself as thin as possible. Within feet of striking me, they parted—passing around me in coordinated communication with each other, merely brushing past me. Despite the power of their wildness, they instinctively chose gentleness. As the herd protected me, I felt that our spirits bonded. We share the land with mutual respect. We are both powerful and fragile. That experience changed my sense of responsibility to steward the land and its creatures.

My desire to live on a glacier and learn to do so safely brought me to the Kahiltna Glacier along the buttresses to Denali. Our team of five was roped together tentatively traversing snow bridges over deep crevasses. The glacier was an immense volume of rock and ice. It was gorgeous, and so quiet. When one of us fell into a crevasse, the rest of the line arrested the fall, working together to extricate the stricken climber. The fiercely self-reliant individuals were absolutely committed to working together to survive and enjoy the beautiful adversity. With each day, our teamwork was more efficient and our trust grew. The conversation changed at camp. Climbers shared life stories and problems, assisting each other with solutions. Our successful confrontation of nature's adversity fostered the confidence to overcome social barriers, applying the teamwork to confrontation of personal adversity.

Steve and I have ridden hundreds of miles together on our bicycles—through day and night and sunny farmland, but mostly through fierce winds and torrential rain. When I needed help, Steve drafted for me. He encouraged me. He taught me the team approach to managing the demanding physical endurance and adverse weather. As had been true backpacking on the tundra, I felt a bonding of spirits. As had been true on the glacier, the successful confrontation and enjoyment of physical adversity enabled a new trust in exploring personal and professional adversity. We seized upon our rides as an opportunity. The simultaneous encounter of the difficult physical and personal challenges enhanced success in both.

Nature is inspirational in its beauty and dangerous in its adversity. It is a catalyst for self-discovery and growth in relationships. In these ways it nurtures learning and leadership. Nature is forever a medicine for the psyche and the soul.

Bio

Cary S. Keller, MD, FACSM is Medical Director at Sportsmedicine Fairbanks. He trained as an orthopedic surgeon specializing in sports medicine and knee reconstruction at Carleton College, University of Chicago, and the Olympic Medical Training Site in Cincinnati. He is team physician for the University of Alaska Fairbanks and for the Fairbanks North Star Borough School District. Dr. Keller serves as chair, fellow, and trustee on a number of committees including the American College of Sports Medicine and the Western Collegiate Hockey Association. He is active in the development and implementation of legislation addressing concussions and sudden cardiac arrest in student athletes.

Pleasurable Terror for a Cause

~ Learning nature's lessons through
full exposure to her ferocity ~

Cancer is an ugly, heartless beast, taking individuals and scarring families indiscriminately. Its victims might be weak or strong, wealthy or needy, urban or rural, young or old, famous or unknown. During my University of Alaska Fairbanks tenure, we hosted Susan Butcher's memorial service on campus. Susan, a Boston native, Fairbanks-based Alaska musher, won the Iditarod four of five years during her reign. Susan and her family occasionally attended events on our campus. She entered life three years after I did and died in 2006. Cancer did not notice that this remarkable athlete was tough as nails, unstoppable, and relentless in pursuit of victory through Alaska's wilderness. Cancer did not care that Susan left behind a wonderful husband and two young daughters. Cancer took no notice that Susan's friends included the likes of George Lucas and Bill and Melinda Gates, all of whom attended the service. I despise cancer's cold indifference.

I thought of Susan, David, Tekla, and Chisana as I biked more than 500 miles over the three Urbana years I participated in Relay for a Reason, raising awareness and money for the American Cancer Society. My miles aggregate from repeated ten-mile loops on a paved rail to trail, each lap refreshed by a stop at Urbana University's student center. Susan's annual 1,000-mile Iditarod covered extreme wilderness, punishing days punctuated by nights of caring for the dogs and grabbing too-little shuteye. Susan was tough. Cancer is tougher.

Susan's adventures could not have been more nature-based. She and the dogs could not have been more immersed in the natural world. I am convinced that she could have added much to the notion of nature-inspired learning and leading. Yet I can't ask her. I can only access my memory of her as I reflect on this second ride through the night, and recall long conversations with David after Susan passed.

This second ride imposed the pleasurable terror (pleasurable only upon reflection) over miles and hours of wild weather. I recall times during that long night when rain washed tears from my cheeks as I reflected on Susan and others whom cancer has taken. My original reflections offered verbatim below did not record those deep emotional and personal observations. I can only resurrect vague snippets from a now five-year-old memory. A lot has happened since then. As with the other two rides, I will draw some nature-inspired lessons in closing.

I'm typing this about 24 hours after the end of a 167-mile, 20-hour, Rally for a Reason adventure. My recollections can't distinguish clearly among the many 10-mile laps that took me through the evening Friday, into a night of wild wind and rain. Finally, night yielded to a day that dawned beautifully and meekly, only to fade quickly into clouds, wind, and rain just as I ran out of gas mid-morning. Because all of us at Urbana University share in the fight to defeat cancer, I am offering reflections, observations, and revelations from the rally.

I begin by thanking the following categories of supporters:

- Those who pledged more than $2,500 for cancer and our UU Wellness Program
- Intrepid faculty, staff, students, and friends, co-riders all, who variously enjoyed the mild start or braved the wild darkness.

Last year I covered two ten-mile laps alone; this year at least one companion graced every lap!

- Campus community members who cheered the start, observed our occasional passage as each lap ended and a new one began, and the kind crowd greeting the final return to campus with noisy appreciation and greeting

Individual sponsors provided a list of more than 20 friends, family members, or colleagues who have dealt—or are dealing with—cancer, some successfully, others not. I took my own and these adopted memories with me through the ride, reminding myself constantly that life and health are precious and vulnerable. That friends and family are irreplaceable. That every day is a gift and that every hug could be the last one. I reminded myself that every smile is priceless. I remembered that sacrifice and effort for a cause yield immeasurable dividends to the soul and psyche.

Our students who rode from one to five laps brightened the journey and lifted my spirits. I hope I didn't miss anyone, but I admit that fatigue dulls the brain cells.

Dr. Cary Keller takes the prize for traveling farthest to participate. Cary is our dear friend and team physician from the University of Alaska Fairbanks. He covered some 60 miles in his first ride of the season (with a Fairbanks snowpack still at 18 inches). Dr. Keller spent more than three hours on campus Thursday with our athletic training students in lecture and conversation. One of our AT students spent 10 bicycle miles Friday with him in deep career conversation.

Local businesswoman Kay McOwen gets the prize for getting me through the wee hours. She arrived on the scene at 2:00 AM during a pounding rain, and spirited me to the finish line mid-morning. About an hour before daybreak we began an abbreviated lap after seeing a blood-red radar return approaching from the southwest. Rather than embarking on a ten-mile loop, we circled nearby neighborhoods watching lightning closing in and hearing the thunder rumbling ever closer. We reached the safety of the student center about three minutes before the fury arrived, grateful that radars tell no lies.

Within two weeks of the start I had actually believed that covering 200 miles was within the realm of possibility. A week out, when the long range forecast hinted at "an energetic system lifting out of the southwest," I saw 200 fading. During the wild night, I kept telling myself that I had until noon, the official end-time, to reel in 160. In the early morning, battling the wind during the 13th lap, I dreaded facing three more to achieve 160. Kay coached, mentored, cajoled, and challenged me to buck it up and keep pedaling.

The deepest, darkest segments of the journey began with lap eight. By then, a steady rain delivered by a gusty breeze yielded to lighter rain, as the breeze increased to a howling gale. The southerly trek from The Depot to Cedar Bog bore into the wind, causing us to gain purchase only with great effort. Where the wind crossed us along an open one-mile stretch, we struggled to maintain balance, leaning uncomfortably to the left into its force. At one point I decided that any worsening would force us to stop the ride. During the strongest winds, each stop at the Cedar Bog turnaround offered us a pause to listen to the roar, whine, and angry groans of the gusts; we were struck by a fear and respect that must be hard-wired.

I likened the wind's power and fury, the darkness, the seeming presence of evil, and the uncertainty to the menace that is cancer. How frightening it must be! In reality, we reminded ourselves, we were in no immediate danger with the safety of the student center only five miles ahead. Northbound, we enjoyed the merciful tailwind, the kinder side of the punishing gale that made the trip out so frightfully difficult. As in life, every dark cloud has its silver lining. Spring's warmth, beauty, and renewal follow even the deepest winter.

The wind eased as the rain returned in our tenth lap. We found it tough to leave the student center for lap 11; the radar showed hours of rain still to come and we could hear it pounding on the skylights. The downpour accompanied the entire lap. We could not have been wetter. Upon return we shed our soaked gear and replaced it with dry clothes, knowing that the rain would greet us when we departed for lap 12. But by then Kay had arrived and, with her, some good luck. The radar revealed that a huge batch of impending greens and bright yellows had parted, giving us a dry slot that could offer a couple laps without rain. We hit the road without delay. The wind, albeit at less than full fury, had returned, this time as a welcome drying agent.

Lap 13 brought the first tentative birdsong, trilled by a feathered friend with deep faith that dawn was somewhere east of sight. And, lap 14 followed the thunderstorm ushering in a long-awaited dawn; it was rich with welcome and the growing certainty that the 160-mile target was within reach. We found new energy on our final lap, racing the wind northward from Cedar Bog, and gliding from Grimes to our student center finish.

Our campus Friday afternoon and evening stayed alive with activities. I enjoyed seeing so many students and staff participating. Music filled the student center and quad until midnight. Healthy Kids Day staff and volunteers began arriving before 7:00 AM, and an hour later we fatigued bikers were lost among hundreds of kids, parents, and supporters, hosted by our entire football team, standing out brightly in their jerseys. The beehive of activity reminded us that a new day follows the darkest of nights, that hope and promise are often just around the bend. We realized once more that our university is a vibrant community center, and it humbled me that all of this positive energy and remarkable commitment took place while the university's president was on a bike, invisible to the folks who were making the day possible.

I hope that our ride served as a symbol that preparation, dedication, team effort, and selfless service can accomplish a great deal. We rode (collectively) well over 500 miles, having "fun" and drawing attention to a disease that is relentless, indiscriminate, and deadly. We reminded ourselves and others that health, wellness, and fitness are necessary (but not sufficient) to a life well-lived. Again, I thank everyone who made our Rally for a Reason successful and rewarding. Finally, I am thanking my wife Mrs. Jones for spending the entire night as our pit crew: tirelessly serving soup, cookies, pizza, fruit, dry towels, encouragement, empathetic words, smiles, and a hug or two as needed.

My relationship with nature is rooted inextricably in weather. How can one experience nature fully in only fair weather? Thus, I am grateful for that night of wind, rain, lightning, and pleasurable terror. Alfred Noyes knew the wind and darkness, painting it perfectly in 1913 with the first stanza of *The Highwayman*:

> "The wind was a torrent of darkness among the gusty trees. The moon was a ghostly galleon tossed upon cloudy seas. The road was a ribbon of moonlight over the purple moor."

We could only imagine the moon that night five years ago; we would have gladly embraced the trail as a ribbon of moonlight as we went riding, riding, riding. It was the wind as a "torrent of darkness among the gusty trees" that themed our journey. I thought of those words often during that night. We could not avoid the wind's roar, whine, and angry groans. We felt palpable fear and respect, as exposed frail humans in the teeth of nature's fury. Even as I know a tame and docile night would have yielded lessons of a different vein, I must build on what the night actually presented: a panoply of harsh spring conditions accompanying an energetic system lifting out of the southwest.

Literature borrows liberally from nature. In the opening paragraph of her bestselling 1962 novel *A Wrinkle in Time*, Madeleine L'Engle wrote of a night not unlike the one we traversed.

> "It was a dark and stormy night...the trees tossing in the frenzied lashing of the wind. Behind the trees clouds scudded frantically across the sky. Every few moments the moon ripped through them."

Ms. L'Engle reached back to Victorian novelist Edward Bulwer-Lytton's 1830 novel *Paul Clifford* for the dark and stormy night description:

> "It was a dark and stormy night; the rain fell in torrents — except at occasional intervals, it was checked by a violent

gust of wind which swept up the streets, rattling along
the housetops, and fiercely agitating the scanty flame of
the lamps that struggled against the darkness."

Writers have long known that a night like April 15, 2011 affects
readers viscerally, and that a night of pleasurable terror experienced
firsthand strikes indelibly.

The first lesson is this: given a choice, stay indoors when an
energetic system lifts out of the southwest! Given no choice in the
matter, dive deeply into the pleasurable terror and soak it up with
your mind, body, heart, soul, and spirit. Pay attention and experience
it deeply; embed the memory of it, for this is the stuff we tell our
grandkids. That kind of wild weather reminds us that ordinary rainy
days are not worth the energy of complaining.

Nature also teaches us not to sweat the small stuff. Learn to
distinguish nuisance from problem, and problem from disaster.
Embrace adversity as a form of essential calibration. There are also
well-worn idioms that fit, like "into every life a little rain must fall"
and "when it rains, it pours."

Some other lessons emerge. Heading from the dry warmth
of the student center into the storm proved far easier with riding
companions. Colleagues and fellow travelers ease the burden of any
task under all conditions, but especially when conditions are adverse.
Even now I get chills thinking about the power and fury of the wind
through the trees when we paused each lap at the Cedar Bog parking
area. It's raining, cool, breezy, and dark as I write these words in
New Hampshire. I have not yet retrieved today's mail and newspaper
from some 200 yards down the driveway. These reflections give me
no choice: to not brave these modest elements would amount to an
act of near cowardice compared to what that night demanded of us
every time we mounted for a ten-mile loop. Friends and compatriots
ease the journey, literally and metaphorically.

We also learned from that night as well as from the two other rides that a common cause is a force multiplier. Fighting cancer draws people together. I recall reading somewhere along life's journey that leaders pass through three stages. We begin our professional passage feeling unsure, gaining experience, and feeling a sense of dependence upon those more senior who nurture, guide, and help us learn. Then, for many of us, we become more certain, more cocksure, more absolute that we know the answers, and we strive for and practice independence. Eventually, with deeper experience, we begin to see that such isn't the case. We recognize our own weaknesses; we appreciate that others have strengths that complement ours, and that we need not compete. We see efficiencies and synergies, a growing capacity of the whole. We understand that the pack eats more regularly than the lone wolf. We enter the kingdom of interdependence. We accept and embrace that with the right team, the whole is far greater than the sum of its parts.

I would not have—in fact, *could* not have—pedaled alone through the night. At times, we patterned our single file pedaling after the venerable geese that cover thousands of miles twice each season, spelling one another at the lead, and drafting behind those breaking the gusts. And like the geese, we chatted and announced our pain and joy as we traveled along the old railroad through the Ohio fields and forests. To the observer, we would have seemed as one, just as the skeins of geese ply their migration route in fluid, ever changing, sometimes-noisy formation. Physical support, combined with our shared mission, camaraderie, and the promise of 10-mile breaks spurred us forward into the dark, wind, rain, and impending exhaustion.

I think about my friend Cary who, because of persistent deep snowpack in Fairbanks, had not yet biked that season a single mile in preparation. Yet with our collective effort, he completed six laps. A 60-mile first ride of the year is no small feat. Interdependence: that's the key. Nature has honed the practice across the eons. From the wolf pack to the migrating geese, to a hive of bees or an anthill, to the oak and its mycorrhizal symbiont, interdependence is a hallmark of success and sustainability. Leaders who insist upon doing it solo are temporary leaders doomed to failure.

I draw another observation from Cary's participation. He is an extraordinary, and very busy, professional. He flew 4,000 miles to weather the storm, support his friend's effort, and be there in solidarity to the cause. Cary brought palpable emotional energy to the night. While I may not have tucked in behind him, he led the pack in spirit and heart throughout the night. Every leader must recognize those special people who touch us along the way. Cary is the wind beneath my wings. I can never thank him enough. I will make sure he sees this essay as just one more way of acknowledging his presence in my quest for meaningful living, learning, serving, and leading.

I offer this final reflection. I know that few others share my enthusiasm for pleasurable weather terror. Yet everyone who stayed with me that night felt the same sentiment. We rode with a sense of purpose and common appreciation for the elements. Most of us actually reveled in the wild experience. Teams, I believe, grow stronger through adverse circumstances and shared difficulties. I would enjoy a reunion of those who participated over the three Relay for Life rides. I know our tales and reminiscences would orbit the weather. And, too, we would celebrate the miles covered and the money we raised to fight the cancer monster. Likewise, we would remember the student center breaks of warmth, dryness, and great food.

The lessons for living, learning, serving, and leading include: cherishing shared experience, celebrating the achievement of benchmarks and mileposts, and relishing each moment to those markers. Also, we learned to embrace, recognize, and acknowledge those who make a difference. Too, we paid attention to the journey as much as to the destination; it's the passage that constitutes our lives, not the end.

Perhaps those are not lessons *from* nature. Yet that night, nature indelibly *inspired* the lessons. We were all one with nature. We can never forget that even when we are in our snug beds, we cannot afford to forget nor neglect our dependence upon this one earth. While interdependence describes our preferred relationship with other human beings, our earth relationship must always be one of absolute and utter dependence.

Nature-inspired learning and leading, as well as this series of nature-inspired essays, strives to inspire, educate, and develop leaders (and learners and servers) dedicated to stewarding this one earth in *every* facet of their lives. My hope is that we can encourage and enable some folks to overcome their perennial blindness to our dependence upon this earth. We want to open eyes; to inspire people to look, see, feel and act as informed, conscientious, responsible Earth citizens.

Good-Natured

A Guest Essay by Jeffrey Patnaude

Science has determined that only 10 percent of our genetic potential functions at any given time. The rest of who we can become remains slumbering in our DNA molecules poised for an awakening. What if we were to nudge that potent power from its resting state through the disruption of being good-natured: living with an attitude of thankfulness instead of entitlement, thinking positively, and remembering that all experience has meaning rather? Instead of boredom, what if we discovered awe as the beginning of wisdom and replaced "tolerating change" with "life as a miracle that constantly initiates change." Such implications could radically affect the way we live, work, play, and learn.

If you doubt such simplicity as a solution to the dreary world of depression and exhaustion, walk outside—outside of an incessant busyness that calls for your attention, outside of the emotional drama for which you have purchased season tickets, or outside of a self-pity that has taken up residence in your thinking. Instead, experience the goodness of nature: the renewing energy of what is referred to as "all natural" and breathe in the first breath of an experience of being good-natured.

Good-natured might just be the intended disposition of us as Earth pilgrims who traverse the very planet that gave rise to our birth, whose bones are made from the very dust upon which we walk and whose eyes look upward in search of life meaning from our ancestral stars.

If our workplaces, in which we spend most of our time, were good-natured in their regenerative energy, we might blossom new thinking as the forest spawns opportunity with each budding tree. And when task demands more of our attention than ideation, the continuous flow of the mountain stream is a reminder that process is constant and the focus of our attention can also flow without interruption. We can unify the realms of nature and business because creation is in the business of expression and certainly does not limit itself to only 10 percent of its potential.

Color, flow of energy, and playful imagination are woven through each helical DNA strand just as natural light fills the stage where creation continues in its remarkable stage drama. If we could applaud this act of brilliance and the regenerative power of its creativity, our standing ovation would last throughout eternity: the ultimate rave review. And just as galaxies flow like a river headed for their ultimate destination, our playful ways can channel that same movement of flowing life energy—*"merrily, merrily, merrily, merrily, gently down the stream."*

How we eventually learn these lessons can be taught by our mentor, nature, if we recognize the four seasons of the learning process, moving toward an unconscious competence and a celebration of being eternal learners.

Be good-natured and create beautiful ways to live, work, play, and learn; you will begin to stimulate that genetic code that wants to be fully utilized toward its good-natured destiny.

Bio

Author of seven books on leadership and mentoring and twenty-five children's books, Jeffrey Patnaude is a teacher, speaker, composer, business leader, and Executive Mentor. Recognized as one of the pioneers in bringing together the marketplace and spirit at work, The Patnaude Group's focus and professional dedication for three decades has centered on the most pressing issues facing our culture today. Having trained and mentored over forty thousand business leaders in multiple organizations, Patnaude has been described as "the Leonard Bernstein of leadership development" and has gained an international reputation for his ability to orchestrate environments for transformation.

Two Hundred Mile Reflections

~ Nature best teaches those who engage to the core and test their limits ~

My nature-inspired learning and leading journey interweaves across life, career, and recreational pursuits. Nature touches and defines so much of who I am. I offer a few paragraphs of introduction to a memorable 22-hour experience that ties nature, service, and living to leading.

Our first child, Matt, arrived January 25, 1977. We lived in southeastern Virginia. A field forester for a paper and allied products manufacturing company, I had somewhat recently transitioned into a forest fertilization research position, meaning less time on my feet and in the woods. I decided that I needed to run/jog more routinely; after all, I was getting older, advancing already into the mid-twenties! The day we brought Matt home, I ran a five-mile loop. I recall lying on my back in the lawn afterward, both exhausted and exhilarated. Logging miles religiously, I recorded time, pace, distance, weather, and other elements daily. I totaled the mileage on Matt's 21st birthday. An astonishing 31,000 miles since that day in 1977! Eventually life and mileage exacted a price; my knees called it quits, forcing me to stop running not long after I turned 50.

Because of a deep endorphin addiction from those many exquisite miles, I replaced running with a less-than-perfect substitute: bicycling (outdoor as well as stationary). When we moved to Ohio in 2008, I could access a 200-mile network of paved rails to trail just a quarter mile from our new home. The bike trail passed within a few hundred yards of Urbana University's campus, where I was serving as president. Biking from spring through fall on that magnificent network offered a close substitute to running. What follows is the original text from reflecting on 22 hours in April 2012.

I'll begin these reflections by thanking all donors and riders who supported this third annual bike journey component of Urbana University's Relay for Life! You helped us raise more than $5,000 (we're still accepting ride-related donations) to fight cancer and enhance UU's wellness program. The broader Relay for Life, a campus-wide event that included many activities leading up to and extending from 4:00 PM through midnight Friday, brought the overall total for the fight against cancer to more than $10,000!

My purpose in writing this is to reflect upon the merit, meaning, and effort that resulted in our entire cycling entourage covering north of 1,000 miles, a group effort that spirited me to cross the 200-mile mark (200.1) within the 22-hour announced timeframe. Wild wind, incessant rain, and thunder-squalls marked last year's ride; general peace, tranquility, and only three laps of pesky light rain branded this year's final few laps. Drama and tales of overcoming the elements will not enliven these reflections. Instead, I will focus on some basic truths, realities, and observations from a night on the trail.

We proved the axiom that strength derives from numbers. This year we assembled a full-fledged team. Year one I turned two late night laps riding solo. Last year I did not once play solitaire, but Kay McOwen and I did several fury-engulfed spins as doubles. This year at least five of us rolled every lap! During Friday's daylight hours we rode in small groups, two abreast and engaged in full and continuous conversation. Our vision encompassed a wide field of view and we thrilled with the passing day and sliding landscape. The long night brought focus, intensity, infrequent conversation, and a narrowing perspective. We generally rode single-file, taking turns at leading and drafting, reducing the individual effort and enabling a faster pace. We retracted within ourselves even as we functioned as a single entity. I recall several wee hour laps when I focused only on the spinning tire and flashing taillights of the rider ahead. Riding alone, I never would have covered 200 miles.

Others likewise covered more distance than they thought possible, far exceeding their prior personal best. James Chellis scored a century and a half, 50 miles farther than his prior best. Pastor Dan Leiker hit a century, a hundred percent beyond his record. UU student Andy Stephan went the entire distance with me. Student body president Josh Deans and education honors society member Kevin Fidler turned multiple laps, each setting a personal distance record.

Teamwork manifest far beyond the physical drafting efficiency mechanism. Our late night silent stretches on the trail erupted into high decibel chatter during the student center rests, refreshments, and adjustments. When freshly delivered pizza greeted us a little after midnight we celebrated like school kids! All of us shared common purpose. We occasionally reminded ourselves that we rode for a higher purpose. We knew we were on the trail because the monster that is cancer lurks always in the shadows, having touched (and threatening to strike close again) each of us.

Teamwork surfaced in at least one surprising and meaningful way for me as we neared the 180-mile mark Saturday. I reflected to Andy as we neared the end of a lap that with the rain falling I could be content to call it a day prior to our 10:00 projected finish and short of the magical two hundred. He quietly responded, "Dr. Jones, you can't quit with two hundred within reach, rain or not." Here's the student teaching the educator. I saw the wisdom in his words and recommitted to grabbing the two-hundred-mile brass ring. Teamwork comes in many dimensions.

Urbana University is a comprehensive team enterprise; the ride served as a symbol of all that we do together. Three UU Board members participated: Betsy Coffman shared a lap mid-afternoon Friday; Ben Mitchell hit the trail with us between 2:00 and 3:00 AM, scoring over 50 miles and crossing the finish line with us; Steve

Polsley joined us for an early Saturday daylight lap. Two faculty members, Jacob Daniel and Beth Paul, also helped lighten our load as Friday afternoon members of the team. Multiple students found their way into and out of the circuit, each one adding value and giving all a chance to glimpse the quality and character of our UU students.

There are limits to our ability to stretch ourselves (I suppose we can call it endurance) and still maintain our mental (as well as physical) agility. Because of our winter that was absent much winter-like weather, I had managed to log 1,083 training miles since New Year's Day. Physically, I felt better prepared by far over the prior two years. Regardless, as we penetrated the wee hours, I entered a zone where the physical and mental fatigue began to dull my sense of what was real. Normally quite adept at mental mathematics, I could no longer add the accumulating mileage in my head. My world on the trail occasionally narrowed to only that spinning wheel and the flashing lights. I had difficulty differentiating one lap from another. As we completed one trail segment at The Depot, I recall seeing a police car idling in the parking lot where we turned east onto Miami Street; but later I wasn't sure that I had really seen it. A keen sense of reality reemerged for me when the first birds began chirping pre-dawn. They lifted my spirits and removed the veil of vagueness that had closed over me when the mid-morning finish seemed so distant. Often in life, the fatigue of stressing, coping, and persevering can impose its will on us, blurring our ability to function, differentiate, and see the finish line. In fact, so much of what we all experienced across the miles has multiple lessons for life.

In response to hearing of our venture, a friend jokingly asked why we would ride through the night just to end up where we started. He said, "I think I would rather just take a seat." I responded to his email with the following words: "Ah, but you miss the point. It's not so much the travel through space but the passage through time that matters. Life itself is a journey through time, rewarded here and there by spatial sojourns, but providing the deepest payback via the people, experiences, joys, and achievements that mark the way. Those nearly 22 hours furnished deep dividends, to include the shifts from daylight to dusk to dark to dawn to full day again, a pattern that no matter how many times I experience it, still provides exhilaration beyond compare. I plan to take a seat when I die. Living richly and deeply does not involve taking a seat!"

I want to offer a few special acknowledgments. I already mentioned Andy's efforts and inspiration. James Chellis packed his bike east from Santa Cruz to log one hundred fifty miles; we talked business (UU is partnering with his company Comcourse on online education), dreams, and aspirations. Ben Mitchell drove ninety minutes to engage with us from the wee hours on; his wife Paula came along and provided additional pit service support. Kay McOwen accompanied us (actually she set the pace and led the way over many laps) for the final one hundred twenty-five miles; what a great friend and absolute trooper! Peggy Kessler selflessly gave the entire night to pit crew duties, helping Judy last the entire night. Judy once more provided the wind beneath my wings, as she has done through our own forty-year marital journey!

I can't imagine how we can top this two hundred-mile, $5,000 feat next year. I know we will have even greater participation. We discussed some ideas over the miles. I am intrigued with the notion of making it a true relay, with one crew departing every time the prior group completes a lap, thus avoiding the very necessary down time for a single team between laps. We could take pledges not just for the miles that Steve covers, but for the total accumulated relay laps. Had we done that this year I feel certain we could have approached three hundred miles (we averaged 14.1 miles per hour while we were in the saddle pedaling those two hundred miles). I see us extending the time to an even 24 hours. I envision an outdoor fire pit with chairs for the resting riders, maybe some midnight s'mores!

Again, thank you participants and donors, team members all! We broke new ground and did our small part against the evil foe that is cancer. We demonstrated that the whole is greater than the sum of its parts. We reached deep inside and stretched ourselves. We created memories. We tested our muscles, our minds, and our hearts. We accepted a challenge and lifted each other. We had fun!

I write these supplemental comments now nearly five years since The Epic Ride. I left Urbana University to assume my Antioch University New England presidency before the next year's Relay for Life, so the big plans did not materialize. The memory lives on. So how does The Ride offer lessons for nature-inspired learning and leading?

First, so many of us are blind to the magic and wonder that surrounds us, envelops us, and truly blesses us; if only we would open our eyes and look! And not just "look," but soak up those surroundings with every sense: sight, sound, scent, touch. If we could absorb our environment with every portal (mind, body, heart, soul, and spirit). Experience every moment. Pay attention. What a mystical night we had in 2012! Riding quietly through the night sates far more than just an optical appetite. When I focused occasionally on the spinning tire in front of me, I threw off the shackles of processing overwhelming visual messages. I pedaled and listened, felt, smelled, and enjoyed the night. I can close my eyes now and find myself reliving every sensory and spiritual sensation: wind, dampness, spring peepers, darkness beyond the headlight, and crystal twinkles above.

The long hours and relentless miles demanded that I accept and embrace the night. Such should be the same for any workplace, life, or service commitment. I've seen too many people pass blindly through the hours. What is the reward in that? I've watched people walk along the shore with ear buds. What could be sadder than silent surf? I've seen young couples sharing a meal while both exercise their thumbs feverishly on handheld electronic devices. What could be more tragic than the lost intimacy of eye-to-eye conversation?

We hone our sensory "muscles" through use. I find that the most effective sensory workout derives from nature: it's real, in the moment, full sensory immersion. It's as accessible in the corporate courtyard as in backcountry wilderness. Practice sensory immersion, whether in urban "wildness" or in a national wilderness. Learn to pay attention. In the backcountry, such attention is necessary to survival. In business, paying attention is just as necessary to thriving...and to enjoying.

Second, I reach back to the metaphor of that journey through the night, when I responded to my skeptical friend who questioned the ride to nowhere. I've spent nights in airports, reeling in sensory deprivation; nature is far more generous, entertaining, and rewarding. My airport nights—fortunately infrequent occurrences—added little to my life's treasured memories, and somehow failed to inspire my living, learning, serving, and leading. Yet even those painfully extended hours on the bike provided a lesson: always count the blessings that I too often take for granted. Nature nourishes me; reminds me that ours is a journey through time, and that each moment matters.

The darkest hour is just before dawn is a tried and true metaphor. I experienced it literally and metaphorically late that night, mentally and physically exhausted. The birdsong that greeted me after the long darkness of night is a signal of ultimate faith and hope. The bird knows the dawn is at hand. I suggest that faith is integral to effective leadership: faith in ourselves, in our team, in our cause. Faith is not blind hope. Instead, faith is steeped in knowledge, experience, and preparation. Faith derives, too, from a belief in something larger, whatever that might mean to each of us.

Yet late that night my faith nearly gave way to fatigue, persistent light rain, and temptation. Had Andy not kindly boosted my weakening will I might have stopped pedaling altogether. The student taught the educator: a reminder that the team enables so much, that every member of the team is essential, that the leader often follows. The ecosystem of life, business, society, and family is founded in interdependence. The student lifted the president. The mycorrhizal partnership enables the oak tree. There is no such distinction as "the least among us." Living, learning, serving, and leading demand interdependence. Whether an oak drawing strength and sustenance from a fungal symbiont or the pedaling president from an undergraduate fellow rider, leadership requires recognizing and drawing upon each member of the team. Leadership means resisting going it alone.

I ask myself, does a ride through the night translate to these lessons as deriving from nature? I suppose there could be lessons drawn from a group of colleagues enjoying a night at the bowling alley. Or an extended evening of poker. Or closing down the saloon within dawn's reach. However, I would not find the full dose of inspiration from those endeavors to last the night. It is only nature that is so richly stimuli-laden, along with steady and demanding physical exertion that could propel me through the wee hours, readying me to burst into the dawn. It is only nature that would engage all five of my sensory portals. It is only nature that could inspire the vast array of lessons I see and discover through outdoor immersion. I am a night owl only in the great outdoors. Otherwise, I operate diurnally.

Nature's night serves me well and enriches my life, even as it strengthens my leadership philosophy and attitude. Add friends, colleagues, marathon-level exertion, and a degree of challenge, and the result is yet another lesson in humility and inspiration: essential elements for effective leadership. Such a ride does not define nature's wisdom. Instead, those 22 hours inform my understanding of the concept of *applying* nature's wisdom; the Epic Ride opened my eyes and head to better understanding and interpreting the possibility that nature could instruct, guide, and inspire how we live, learn, serve, and lead. And I am heartened to revisit these five-year-old reflections to see that what now has a name—"nature-inspired learning and leading"—had already begun to take shape in my mind.

In fact, my entire life's journey has been trekking slowly and inexorably toward embracing the notion of nature-inspired learning and leading. I'm comforted to discern that this concept of nature expressing and inspiring essential lessons is not a flash in the pan: a wild idea emerging from my aging mind. I have been following this path for decades, unaware of the destination that is nature-inspired learning and leading. Each of these reflective essays offers me a deeper look into the emerging discipline, and opens my mind to yet another swing through my past, eyes growing more alert to lessons formerly hidden to my closed eyes.

Nature-inspired learning and leading is a new way of looking, seeing, feeling, and acting. I am grateful for the luxury of combining incredible experiences in nature, filtered through my natural sciences education and training, and interpreted and applied via my commitment to more responsibly live, learn, lead, and serve. Likewise, I am blessed to have had the bully pulpit as a university president (and now as a former university president) to record and publish these ruminations. Life is good, satisfying, and rewarding. I am applying my trade and preaching the gospel of responsible Earth stewardship. I will have succeeded if only a handful of leaders, present and future, understand and embrace the concept and practice of nature based and nature-inspired leadership.

> "Great ideas originate in the muscles."
> Thomas Edison

Learning from a Frog Pond

~ Learning from nature, whether on a grand scale or in some small way ~

Nature-inspired lessons derive from nature at many scales: large and small, sweeping and compact. I've combined three essays under the banner of My New Hampshire Frog Pond. I've learned some lessons from the frog pond. Lessons and inspiration that fit well within this series of essays on nature-inspired learning and leading.

The Original Frog Pond Essay
February 21, 2014

We've made eleven interstate moves in our 42 married years: we came *home* June 2013 to a place we'd never lived before. We moved to a place not far from Keene, NH where I now serve as president of Antioch University New England, an institution that focuses to a significant degree on natural resources and sustainability: my disciplinary roots.

We've bloomed wherever we were planted, but this feels different—special. As a forester, for me nothing beats living in the country's most heavily forested state. Our four acres of heaven-on-Earth encompass several hundred feet of New England stone walls running through the dense second growth that reclaimed land cleared 200 years earlier by intrepid Europeans intent upon taming the wilderness. When more fertile ground beckoned from the Ohio Valley and beyond, walled-in pasture yielded to inexorable succession: brush to forest. The walls now border and interweave among seeming-ceaseless forest, stretching from one abandoned homestead to thousands more.

And our 1770 home survives—since dismantled beam by beam and post by post in 1993 and reassembled—a quarter of a mile north of where it graced the hillside for two centuries. Since late June last year, we've watched summer peak and ebb; fall gain footing, flourish, and fade; and winter grab tight and build a 30-inch snowpack. In fact, winter held sway over our entire four-acre domain. Except for one 12x15 foot element of resistance, a spot on the landscape that refused to yield to the icy grip! I'll explain below.

Our home sits forty vertical feet above our township road, with mowed grass and beds sloping east to the thirty-foot-wide forest edge bordering it. We've honed our landscaping attack plan over our multiple moves, and began an aggressive campaign immediately: three intended stages before the snow flew. First, we're not big on grass; we would convert as much grass to perennial and shrub beds as we could manage. Second, we wanted to include a dry-stack stone wall or two to terrace and highlight areas of the property. Third, we decided to eliminate the invasive buckthorn that had captured a fifteen-to-thirty-foot swath of clearing along most of the south and west sides, steadily encroaching and blocking our view into the forest. Each task warrants a separate essay at another time.

The fourth project is the topic of this essay.

Beyond the small (yet year-round) stream that runs diagonally across our forest and then along our driveway, we cleared the thickest of the buckthorn. I stumbled into (and then avoided) a depression filled to the brim with water-laden organic debris, looking at the surface like a flat spot of leaf-covered forest floor. Instead, the leaves yielded to decades of muck as deep in the center as eighteen inches. Frogs claimed the entire stream length, and I noticed many more at the depression, leaping into the muck when disturbed.

Why is there a eutrophic *pond* (meaning it's too big and permanent to be a puddle or vernal pool) just twenty feet beyond our stream, and a couple of feet higher? I decided to do a little ecologic and geomorphic sleuthing. My doctoral research long before had evaluated soil-site relationships in the Allegany hardwood forests of northwest Pennsylvania and southwest New York, an area typified by pit and mound topography. Imagine a large tree buffeted by winds, toppling over, roots ripping from the earth, pulling a large volume of soil along with them, creating a pit where the soil lifted. Eventually, the wood (root, trunk, branches) decays, leaving only the evacuated pit and the elongate (axis perpendicular to the direction of fall) mound of soil. Creating our pond, a three-foot-high mound (the direction of fall paralleling the stream) supports beech, maple, and hemlock up to ten inches in diameter. The fallen giant has long since decayed.

But here's the puzzle: why does this particular pit hold water year-round? I decided to answer that question and at the same time determine whether I could convert the muck hole to standing water, and enhance my amphibian friends' haven. So the mucking began in late summer 2013. I made the task initially tougher than needed. I shoveled the heavy, water-laden organic debris into five-gallon buckets, and then carried them to add richness to a new terraced bed more than a hundred feet away. Dozens of buckets later, struggling in and with the muck, I shifted to shoveling to the edges. Throughout the three-weekend project, frogs began to show in greater numbers. As muck yielded to very muddy water, clear water began gurgling from the upslope side, seeming to bubble from the ground. The next morning's visit showed me that it had become crystal clear. Frogs hopped in as I approached, sometimes a dozen or more. And then I began seeing a salamander or two on the silt-covered bottom. My efforts ceased about then and fall weather dissuaded the frogs from venturing into the uninviting air. I thought about how winter would freeze the surface and protect my amphibious friends from winter's fury.

But there was still another mystery. It was the coldest winter in decades, and still our pond supported no ice. Our stream froze over in late December, its voice silent beneath the deep snow and ice. We're not in a true thermal groundwater zone. The recharge I witnessed while mucking does not appear rapid enough to resist freezing, even if the flow is artesian and much warmer than my stream's surface water. We'll solve this some other day.

We're eager for the ultimate response to mucking: will we have created an amphibian nursery? What does the spring hold for them and us? For now, please reflect with me on whether you are taking real and palpable sustainability steps to make a difference during your own journey through life.

The Second Frog Pond Essay: After the Solstice End of June 2014

We've now passed the summer solstice. The frog pond I mucked out from a wet, organic detritus-laden depression last fall is now in its summer state. My February 2014 musings about the pond puzzled over the "ultimate response to mucking." This piece is my reflection from my frog-pond-neighbor perspective (the "us") of what the mucking did for "them," the pond residents.

Because the pond surface never froze, even during the coldest winter in decades, I did not need to wait for the ice to disappear, although the snow stayed under the surrounding forest canopy until early April. In fact, the snow still surrounded our pond when the spring peepers already filled the air with evening and night song from wet depressions in open meadows just a few hundred yards away. My little pond friends remained silent for weeks after that, although on warmer days I saw a few leap from the shore into the pool as I approached. I was beginning to panic. Had my mucking last fall disrupted life enough to depress amorous amphibian ambitions? What have I done to my friends?

As it turned out, I had done nothing negative. I pulled into the driveway mid-May in the early evening. My heart raced when I heard the first distinctive "peep" from the wood's edge. Over the next week, the long awaited "peep" grew to a cacophony. The chorus evidenced some happy critters, focused appropriately on what spring prompts for many of God's creatures! Within days I saw gelatinous egg masses, holding place in the thickening algae that appeared almost as suddenly as the peeping. I'm now seeing tadpoles, and when I visit the pond, a dozen or more frogs leap into the water. That's far more than I saw a year ago, before my fall mucking.

That's all well and good. However, several questions and concerns now challenge me.

- The algae. The pond seems filled with the stuff. Is it choking life in the pool? Is it enriching life? What am I missing by not being able to see through it? Well, I took to the web. I perused the Internet for explanations and experiences that others might share. Several advised that even most natural ponds and pools are not sparkling clean. Accumulated organic matter is a natural condition that encourages the critters that frogs and their tadpoles eat. Algae is another source of cover, nourishment, and desirable habitat for the frog pond ecosystem.

- Winter-accumulated debris. I can see from this winter's accumulation of organic debris how the pond filled over the course of a decade or more. From mid-fall—when I completed mucking—to the first warm days of spring, the accumulation tempted me to begin immediate removal. I thought better for two reasons. First, though the days were mild, the water felt frigid; I had no desire to ruin an otherwise beautiful day outdoors. Second, I saw many signs of life and felt that serious disturbance would have upset the spring awakening process.

Adding the above advice regarding the favorable role of organic matter, I decided to delay action, if any, to after the fall leaf drop. I know that by then the critters will be at rest, hibernating in the very debris I am wishing gone.

- Frog predation. I'm not concerned about what might be eating the frogs; the population seems to be flourishing. Instead, based upon the number of egg masses, I am concerned that my tadpole numbers fall far below what I believe should be apparent. Once again, I went to the web, where Amphibian and Reptile Groups of the UK reported,

"Of course, the reason that frogs lay so many eggs is that very few survive into adulthood—usually only a handful from each original clump."

That gave me hope that my pond is a safe haven for amphibian breeding and rearing their young. I also visited another site seeking a second opinion; it indicated that the odds are not in favor of a tadpole living long enough to become a frog. Tadpoles are so low on the totem pole that even dragonfly larvae and other predatory insects frequently make a meal of them. And pollywogs aren't even safe from their own family members: frogs often eat tadpoles, and big tadpoles sometimes swallow smaller ones." I wondered if I should name the pool "Donner Pond." Once again, I cycle back to yet another reason for welcoming the debris and algae. Tadpoles are not known for their speed and agility; that organic matter burden—a negative for my aesthetic eye—harbors my low-on-the-food-chain guests.

- Salamanders. I haven't seen a single salamander this early summer season; I confirmed at least two at one time last fall. That sighting was through clear and debris-free water; now I cannot see the bottom, where they had rested, except for an occasional peek through the algae, not unlike flying above a mostly full cloud cover and once in a while seeing the ground through a small break. I will assume that they still inhabit the pool and are hidden beneath the rich clouds of algae and organic debris. Upon viewing salamander egg mass photos via Google, I see that some of the egg masses could very well be salamander eggs.

I'm humbled by how little I know! I take solace that I can still learn. And I will learn. I will watch the seasonal cycles. In this land of four distinct and deep seasons, life cycles with the sun's journey.

The sun's heat and energy; the ebbs and flows of moisture; the life, death, activities of all creatures (flora and fauna); and so much more constitute the cycles. What a pleasure to see and appreciate the beauty and bounty up close and personal.

I have one remaining dilemma: do I manage my pond? And if so, how often or to what effect? I'm making a case (in my words, observations, and leanings expressed above) for a somewhat hands-off approach. I'm still not sure what I will do. Dealing with nature is never simple; layers of complexity run deep. My instinct—rooted in decades of natural resources management experience—signals that less is more. Until I am persuaded beyond where I now stand, I will not cleanse my pool of the detritus.

I'm closing these thoughts while appreciating the deepening greens of the interrupted, cinnamon, and hay-scented fern glade near the pond at the edge of the woods. I deeply wonder what mysteries and gifts lie there beyond sight and beneath my understanding.

The Third Frog Pond Essay: The Fourth Summer
August 4, 2016

Now to the fourth season of our *former* frog pond. I admit to a few distractions as a weak winter led into an early spring that only reluctantly yielded to deep spring and summer. Yet I found relaxation and solace in winter visits, awaiting the first spring vocals, celebrating the season's first egg mass appearance (eventually nine), seeing tadpoles emerge, and watching adults leap into the pool every time I approached.

Winter managed to produce limited and not very persistent snowpack. Maximum depth may have reached a foot, just 40 percent of the prior winter. Subnivian critters never enjoyed the long protection from predators afforded by the preceding winter's 2.5 feet. Our ornamental plants likewise missed the deep snow cover that protects them. With just a few inches, the temperature in our wooded location dipped to 16 degrees below zero. We lost one hydrangea and two azaleas. Our hellebores died back to ground level.

Regardless, once more, the frog pond did not freeze. Over our three winters, we witnessed only a little pond margin ice—and that only occasionally. I will never entirely solve the mystery of why the tiny water body did not freeze. I intended to monitor its temperature. My good intentions seldom give way fully to actualization. The only advantage of not monitoring and measuring is that now I can accept my conjecture without testing and potentially rejecting the hypothesis. My conclusion: the deep forest cover placed a radiational cooling lid over the rich growing medium, and prevented the soil from freezing. Interestingly, northern forest soils that are insulated by a full tree canopy, thick litter, layers of duff, and snowpack seldom freeze.

Another contributing factor is that the groundwater finding the surface at the pond's upper end retained a temperature high enough that its short time in the pool did not bring it below freezing. The physics of heat transfer kept the frog pond ice-free. Nature's laws (physics and heat transfer among them) are fixed, and do not yield to my romantic preference for seeing the pond locked deep in ice.

I should not have been surprised at how much more detritus accumulated this past dormant season. The thick second growth canopy and fertile soil combine to generate tons per acre of leaves and other organic debris. The better-drained soils actively rework the annual debris burden. The pond does not process the organic matter so quickly. It accumulates in ever-deepening layers. Had we remained on that property, I would not yet have acted to reduce the in-pond accumulation. But at some point within the next 3-5 years I believe I would have once again mucked out the pool.

The tadpole population seemed quite reduced this spring. Was it the organic debris reducing my ability to see the larval toads and frogs? Was the burgeoning debris reducing the amphibian carrying capacity? Are there natural ebbs and flows of population at play? Did the never-ending cold spring weather depress hatching and early development? Had I attracted a particularly effective and aggressive predator, to include hungry fellow amphibians?

As with the second year, I saw no salamanders. I found red efts regularly along our road, lifting them from the surface and placing them at the road edge toward which they happened to be oriented. I shall never discern and won't even speculate about why I saw salamanders during the first fall mucking and none the subsequent years.

Once we entertained the house purchase offer, I abandoned my crusade to rid the property of the invasive buckthorn. Fortunately, I had made great progress in converting the near-pond plant community from dense buckthorn to hay-scented, interrupted, and cinnamon fern, and released saplings of hemlock, white pine, red oak, American beech, and quaking aspen. However, were we staying, I would have mounted another buckthorn eradication offensive. I left mid-July with a measure of guilt. I accept some consolation by leaving the new owners a written battle plan that—should they wish to continue the effort—will at least suggest next steps and the associated urgency.

I am a creature of temperate climates, where annual precipitation is generously apportioned across the months. Aside from our time in interior Alaska—where average annual rainfall is approximately eleven inches, we've lived in locales ranging from an annual average of 38-55 inches of precipitation evenly distributed. Prior to this late spring and early summer our NH "stream" (a generous description) had never ceased gurgling and flowing, even during extended dry periods. This year April, May, and June proved very dry. The flow was reduced to just a few wet spots. The gurgling ceased. The frog pond continued to hold water, albeit noticeably less than prior summers. As we prepared to depart, rains began to arrive; perhaps by now, the stream and pond are at more normal summer levels. For the sake of the new owners and our amphibian friends I hope that is the case.

We are now residing more than 1,000 miles away. This was the 11th time we have left behind a patch of earth we loved, tended, and left (in our eyes) for the better. Part of our soul, spirit, and heart remains at each prior location. We carry and cherish the memories. We like to think that some trace of our touch and flair remains, seen and appreciated by others who have followed us, to include the living elements we added with such tender care and thoughtful plan. How will *our* frog pond fare? Will the new owners care? Will the amphibians notice? Did we make a lasting difference? Did our reach extend beyond the mark engrained on our own mind, heart, soul, and spirit? Is that enough?

Although I may not have saved or assisted a single frog friend, perhaps I changed myself in ways that I can pay forward. The most important single lesson that I can draw from this frog pond trilogy is this: we carry a lifelong obligation to make whatever difference we can at whatever scale is available to us, either directly or through those we can instruct, motivate, and inspire.

Some wisdom is ageless and timeless. We are true Earth stewards when we do what we can. We are nature-inspired leaders when we learn from nature, whether on grand scale or in some small way, and apply the lessons learned to living, learning, serving, and leading. Beyond writing about my New Hampshire frog pond, I've employed its lessons in many presentations to students, alumni, donors, and others. I walked many a guest across the short wooden bridge over the stream, to the pool edge, summer and winter. It has served me well. I hope the pond and its residents somehow have considered my care and attention as reciprocal.

Tidal Flats: A Changing-Lives Moment and The Power and Sweep of Nature

~ Emptiness in nature or in living
is merely a state of mind ~

I drafted some portions of this essay in August 2011 while returning to Ohio from a vacation immersion in nature on the Olympic Peninsula and across the strait in Vancouver, BC. Now five years later, as I wrap my head more cogently around the philosophy and practice of nature-inspired learning and leading, I add reflection and commentary: a retrospective interpretation of lessons. Importantly, I draw courage and satisfaction seeing that I had already adopted and discerned many nature-inspired learning and leading threads even then. I'm weaving those threads now into the wonderful fabric that nature's wisdom yields; every other paragraph offers my perspective *today* on those events of half a decade ago.

I'm catapulting along at 39,000 feet, eastbound from vacationing on Washington's Olympic Peninsula. This essay's subject came naturally, spurred by a changing-lives moment for me from a boardwalk trek over the mud flats at Nisqually National Wildlife Refuge near Olympia. Twice-daily tidal fluctuations to 20 feet enrich and enliven this section of the Puget Sound. We had earlier walked along Henderson Bay with longtime friends just as an ebb tide yielded to the initial incoming flush. Arriving at the refuge during another low tide, we saw the boardwalk stretch nearly two miles across vast flats of red mud, a rather stark, lifeless, and empty landscape, or so it seemed.

When we get right down to it, so much we encounter in business, politics, life, and living seems stark, lifeless, and empty. The emptiness dissipates when we learn to deliberately and purposefully look, and then to master the art of truly seeing. Few people even bother to look; they operate blindly. Many others look, but only superficially, seeing little. Looking and seeing must be intentional, disciplined, and practiced.

Closer inspection revealed more. Great blue herons stood expectantly along residual pools and shallow channels, bobbing and tilting, watching for prey and alert for predators. Gulls swooped, laughed, and shrilled, perhaps rejoicing some news not yet revealed to me. Geese stood the higher ground, patient for something they anticipated. Ducks paddled calmly across ponds. A lone immature bald eagle staffed a dead "ghost tree," watching the flats for a sign of a promised meal. I knew the tide would soon cover these flats; I had read the morning's tide tables. After all, I'm a biological scientist; the cycles and rhythms of nature speak to me from textbooks as well as six decades of observation. What I did not know was how the up close and intimate experience of watching the mud flat transform would change my thinking of life and of lives.

We're time travelers, spinning through our lives at 60 minutes per hour. I'll soon have covered 65 years: nearly 570,000 hours. Amazing things have happened in my lifetime: Sputnik and landing on the moon, the Berlin Wall collapsing, the advent of AIDS, the near eradication of polio. I have also witnessed the publication of Rachel Carson's groundbreaking *Silent Spring*, as well as epic environmental strides that include development of the Environmental Protection Agency, the Clean Water Act, the Endangered Species Act, Superfund, and the Resource Conservation and Recovery Act. I have seen the arising of nature deficit disorder, global cooling, and global warming.

I was not prepared for the pace and magnitude of change. The water did not simply rise; it attacked, rushed, forced, and flooded. One thousand acres of tidal flats do not yield easily to ten feet of water. Rivulets sought purchase across ten million points of entry. Tiny flows rose to freshets, and streams grew to rivers as the water rushed to inundate the mud. Bubbles and gurgles gave way to torrents.

A ten-foot tide over one thousand acres flushes and flows 435.6 million cubic feet of water twice daily. That seems like an impressive exchange, yet the average flow of the Mississippi River at New Orleans is 600,000 cubic feet per second. At annual average discharge, the Mississippi could fill Nisqually's tidal flats to ten feet in about 12 minutes. The Amazon River at average flow would take just 55 seconds. Our living Earth is far from static. Wild swings—seasonal, daily, and beyond—define life. Success demands that we understand and anticipate those essential ebbs and flows.

A barren landscape no more, the flats celebrated: herons fished happily, gulls dived and pecked, ducks flew to exploit now extensive water cover, and the eagle took flight likely scouring the water below for the next meal. This magnificent cycle of flooding and renewal occurs twice daily, both imposing and enabling life-giving change.

Our lives flux and surge; dynamic change touches us continuously. How dull life and living would be if every minute of every day offered only constancy. No challenges to overcome. No opportunities to exploit. No dreams to anticipate. No problems to address and no demons to conquer. We find purpose only because nothing is static. The tidal fauna at Nisqually anticipated the twice-daily routine. The daily surges fuel life broadly and deeply. The heron found a meal courtesy of the flux; the heron's meal found death as a result. All of life is a balance of giving and taking. Prey and predator conduct a delicate dance. Even in my former business of higher education, positive and negative shifts and fluctuations abound. Students change over time, technology advances, market demand for our products shifts, our physical plant ages, predators vie for our students, others lure our faculty, we may lose our efficiency and quality edge. Nothing is static; we must anticipate change and make the most of life's ebbs and flows.

Life at times can seem stark, vast, barren, and lifeless. My trek toward Puget Sound revealed otherwise for the mud flats, just as our own passage demonstrates repeatedly that life abounds in ways that nourish, renew, and bless. Life does not simply pass; it surges, forces, and floods. Eighteenth century philosopher Emanuel Swedenborg helped us see and understand that nature reveals lessons, metaphors, and patterns that speak to life and living. He instructed that we watch, listen, and learn from the cycles and rhythms of life and living. The tidal flats opened my eyes to look more closely and thoughtfully to the ebbs and flows around me. What may appear barren, daunting, and hopelessly vast may hold infinite promise for positive change and renewal.

One must always be prepared to walk across the flats with eyes wide open. I could have trekked blindly toward the open water and seen little. Because I have spent a life immersed in nature, I am ever alert to its magic, beauty, and wonder. I know where, how, and why to look. As a result, I see. I see the magnificent whole, even as I discern the intimate detail and rich component stories. I see the weave as well as the full tapestry. That's how all of us should examine the world around us, both natural and otherwise. Nature based leadership instructs and implores us to look deeply, see vividly, feel empathically, and act with passion and purpose. Effective living, learning, serving, and leading demands informed immersion, deliberate attention, and focused observation. Nature-inspired learning and leading offers life-changing inspiration and soul-deepening humility. Try living, learning, serving, and leading without humility and inspiration. What a limpid life such a dull approach yields.

Like the eagle, I have vacated my perch. I am seeking bounty, challenge, reward, and fulfillment in other pools afforded by the dynamism, flux, and surge engulfing me. I know I have a life purpose and that another opportunity will present itself to me. I have invested my life preparing for that next door to open. And like the eagle, I know that opportunity does not come to my perch. That is why the eagle and I have both lifted—our portals open, alert, and eager, willing to search for and accept what we find awaiting us. We will look, see, feel, and then act in pursuit of sustenance and fulfillment.

Crossing the Strait of Juan de Fuca

~ Truly seeing is a matter of perspective ~

So much of living, learning, serving, and leading distills to perspective. We've heard the old saw, "Where you stand depends on where you sit." I draw this essay about perspective from an August 2011 vacation ferry ride. I wrote the original draft a month later en route to China. Herein I have added some additional reflections that offer a broader perspective: that of hindsight.

We view and react to even simple occurrences. Just yesterday, as evening ebbed, I sat on my patio watching an east-west line of developing cumulus (drifting toward the west) begin to drop curtains of tropical rain, and then flash and boom as the rising air and falling torrents generated powerful electrical discharges. I watched from a safe distance of about five miles away from the lightning. I observed with no small measure of envy for those receiving the welcome downpours. We are quite dry here at my home in the Tennessee Valley of northern Alabama. Two mornings prior, I chatted with an heirloom tomato producer at the Madison Farmers' Market, who lamented that the almost daily, relentless tropical showers over his farm were making it difficult to tend and harvest his acres of tomatoes. Last evening's storms tracked repeatedly across those same lands. I watched the showers, feeling hopelessly caught in my localized drought. I am sure my farmer friend viewed his soaked fields with deep concern for the crop and his economic wellbeing. I get off easy, I suppose. I have no economic stake in my drought (other than running the sprinklers a bit more frequently); in contrast, his livelihood is at peril. How we viewed those erupting and tracking storms depended on our individual perspective.

September 17, 2011

Our summer vacation placed us on a ferry heading north from Port Angeles, Washington to Victoria, British Columbia. The trip prompted thoughts about perspective in both time and place. We had gazed from dock across the Strait of Juan de Fuca to the distant shoreline, seeing only a vague outline of hills, without definition. In contrast, Port Angeles dominated our view in strident detail: a marina, shops, homes, warehouses, and a pulp mill with clouds of steam. The nearby hills blocked any view of the Olympic Mountains beyond. The town and harbor odors and sounds likewise filled our senses. We could feel the engines throbbing and awaited our departure; an air horn announced it.

We sat on an upper deck, facing Port Angeles and watching it change. What had been within the harbor now became part of the foreground: boats at anchorage, the spit leading to the Coast Guard station, waves beyond the revetment, and multiple leisure craft underway. At dock, the town occupied our complete width of sight. Quickly our town-subscribed cone of vision narrowed, welcoming shoreline to our view expanding to the west and east. As we pulled away, hills beyond the house-cloaked ridges began to rise, an effect that served to flatten and compress Port Angeles even as the horizontal cone tightened. Detail began to fade; the pulp mill no longer revealed windows, angles, and fences. With time and distance, its entire essence diminished to a steam smudge before it finally became impossible to see at all. The town compressed rapidly, dwarfed by the wide expanse of the expanding viewscape and overwhelmed by the snowcapped beauty of the Olympic Mountains, standing in full and massive splendor.

In time, the Washington coast looked (except for the mountains) much like Vancouver Island had appeared earlier. By then the Canadian shore was beginning to reveal its secrets: individual trees, buildings, flags, boats, the city of Victoria, and great promise for new adventure. Now, some weeks later, both Port Angeles and Victoria exist as memories to us, distilled into a few digital images, enriched by our shared experiences, and sharpened by taking time to record these reflections.

Life is like that: sharp, palpable, real, poignant, and overwhelming one minute then faded and small the next. What lies ahead with great anticipation soon passes behind, leaving impressions, knowledge, and understanding that we take forward to the next moment. We are travelers through space and time—feeling, seeing, knowing, and living most acutely in the moment, yet carrying some hues, tones, textures, and content with us.

I write these words six decades into my own life journey, knowing the sunset is nearer than the long ago sunrise, yet still anticipating, welcoming, and thrilling with each new moment. Although the pace continues at 60 minutes an hour, I believe I'm seeing the countryside a little more clearly these days, filtering the images through eyes enriched by my passage so far. I'm also more inclined to consider the wake I'm leaving behind me: the people I touch, the difference I make in the world. I wonder how I can make this a better place, how I can assist even one person to prepare for their own journey, how I can open eyes to the unnoticed beauty that blesses our unique journey.

My fingers are tapping the keyboard at 38,000 feet, en route to Shanghai for university business. This journey does not afford the luxury of sitting on the upper deck watching O'Hare fall away; the little screen in front of me says that Chicago is already some 6,000 miles behind the plane. The map tells me we are about to enter Chinese air space, certainly new territory for me. I know that the magic and wonder of an exotic land and people await me. I know, too, that I have just seven days on the ground to soak it in, make a difference, and build memories. I'm both eager and anxious about what I will encounter. I know life lessons will reveal themselves to me if only I am seeking. I vow to stay alert for them. That much I've learned from other journeys.

August 2016

Even that trip to China has faded with time. In the moment, I assumed one overriding purpose: to represent the university I led and served, and to explore opportunities for partnerships and recruitment. I focused on contact names, program details, shared objectives, and possibilities. That is why I traveled there. Fortunately, I recorded other thoughts as well: impressions, feelings, observations of people and place, and indelible memories captured by mind, heart, spirit, soul, and body. Even without retrieving the written notes, I can close my eyes and see the Great Wall, feel the sting of Beijing's acrid smog, and hear the teeming streets in Shanghai. My perspective as I pause to reflect is nature based. I no longer care about the partnership and recruitment elements.

I am buoyed to discover that the memories remain palpable, and heartened that I recall them within the context of nature-inspired learning and leading and Earth stewardship. Perspective varies across time, distance, and the seasons and focus of life and work. I would like to return to China now wearing my full nature-inspired metaphorical and intellectual regalia. To take along the lenses through which I now view so much. However, this wee exercise of contemplating the role of perspective, revisiting the short journey across the Strait of Juan de Fuca, awakened me to the wonderful realization that I can make that return trip to China through the portals of memory, and with the help of my written notes. Nothing could truly substitute for a physical return to China. However, I am now on a fixed income, and do not have the compelling employer-based impetus to forge revenue-positive partnerships. Perhaps one day I will make new memories and gather fresh perspectives.

Where we stand does indeed depend upon where we sit. Yet when I visited China in 2011 I had already adopted the concept of nature-inspired learning and leading, even though I had not named it. I was subconsciously looking, seeing, and feeling along the lines that have evolved since then to constitute the notion of applying nature's wisdom to life and work. I had disciplined myself to awareness, filed the memories, and consulted them occasionally as example and metaphor.

Oddly, I am now rethinking my crossing of the strait. Rather than the competing perspectives of departing one port and arriving at another, I now view it as simply the crossing from the perspective of five years hence. I see it as a reminder that perspective is simply one element of living. Nature-inspired learning and leading instructs and reminds us that everything is perspective oriented. Are we the producer or the consumer? Are we buying or selling? Coming or going? Here...or there? Are we doing...or being done to? Are we on the boat...or sitting at the dock watching the boat set sail? Are we contemplating what lies five years ahead...or recalling the crossing from five years hence? It's all relative. It's all perspective-based.

Nature-inspired learning and leading stimulates us to consider where we sit: in time, in space, in function, in relationship to all else. Where do we sit in nature's web of life? John Muir observed,

> "When we try to pick out anything by itself, we find
> it hitched to everything else in the universe."

Where we are "hitched" is both real as well as a matter of perspective. Nature's wisdom reminds us that all things are interconnected. Perspective enables us to distinguish the ways that all things fit, and especially where we as individuals—and as a species—fit.

The Seamlessness of Breath and Urge

A Guest Essay by Jennifer J. Wilhoit

Inspire: 1. fill with the urge or ability to do or feel something, especially to do something creative.

2. breathe in (air); inhale.

To live is to breathe and create. To live a nature-inspired life is to recognize our oneness with the world of nature, allowing that unity to animate and permeate everything we do.

When I am profoundly fatigued by the weight of global issues we endeavor to positively address day by day; when I carry stress; when I have a complex problem to work through; when I need a respite, a break, or some spiritual rejuvenation…I go out into nature. I go out into the enriching, insightful, replenishing, enlivening raw outdoors. I go out with my dilemmas and weariness, and I pause. I close my eyes; I slowly inhale. I breathe in the fresh scent of lilacs in spring, decaying leaves in late fall, sun-warmed grass in July, redcedar boughs in a brittle winter wind. And my corpus, my emotional body, my mind, my spirit are slowly rewoven back into the fabric of wholeness. I remember how to call on the wisdom of that interconnection. I go back into the world, after a time of reflection and restoration, able to reengage all that is my calling; I exhale my gifts as a soft breath, as a balm, in service to the needs around me.

I breathe in the natural world in order to live, to learn, to guide others from an energized place of inspiration. I am inspired by the limitless possibility for growth that nature teaches us. I am inspired by her beauties, cycles, and patterns. I inspire others by offering them an opportunity to see their own lives in a more interconnected, multifaceted way.

This has been my pattern throughout my life:

I need limberness; I go hiking in the endless stretch of landscape.

I feel deeply; I go out into nature so that its vastness can hold me.

I desire insight; I go out into the wilds of nature, observe what is there, and learn from it.

I crave spirit; I go out into the bounty of natural landscapes and rediscover the depth of soul in her stones and grasses and salty waters, beside the furred, winged, crawling creatures.

Nature-inspired learning and leading is embedded in who and how I am, in what I do and what I can receive. Nature provides me with the impetus and inclination to create anew: my corpus and the land, acting as one. I remember how to easily step in to the deep work that is my small contribution to the world because I breathe in the scent of earth's soils and seas. It is a flow, this inhalation and exhalation; the boundaries we perceive as "self" and "other" are fabricated. I take comfort in knowing that I am not separate from any other living being on the planet. It is this undeniable and inextricable interconnection that is at the heart of my professional work and that is central to my survival— physically, emotionally, mentally, and spiritually—as a human being.

Bio

Jennifer J. Wilhoit is a spiritual ecologist and the founder of *TEALarbor stories* (www.tealarborstories.com). She earned her Ph.D. in Environmental Studies (people-park conflicts at the edges of protected areas, especially between crafts coops and conservationists), and her MA in Education (environmental, intercultural adult learning). She works as a published author, editor, writing mentor, life guide, mediator, speaker, trainer, educator, researcher, and hospice volunteer. She replenishes herself through hiking, building nature altars, nature photography, reading, collage and painting, travel, and playing in a carillon choir. Jennifer thrives in the beautiful Pacific Northwest landscape in which she lives.

Hurricane Ridge

~ Bending to the cycles of time and events ~

We drove up into the Olympics during the same trip that we visited Nisqually National Wildlife Refuge and then later crossed the Strait of Juan de Fuca. The Pacific Northwest is a dynamic region, blessed with moisture-laden air delivered across a Pacific Ocean fetch of a few thousand miles. Toss in the Olympic Mountains peaking at nearly 8,000 feet to further magnify the region's dynamism. Spectacularly fair and pleasant weather accompanied our time on the Olympic Peninsula. I drafted an essay shortly after the trip, revealing insights and reflections that fit well in this book of essays on nature-inspired learning and leading; this is that original essay. As with hiking the Nisqually NWR boardwalk and crossing the strait, I am pleased that five years ago, I had already embraced and had begun to articulate how I draw strength, insight, and illumination from nature's wisdom.

Even the name evokes ferocity, danger, and power. Contrasting that image, Judy and I visited during a day of absolute tranquility. At more than a mile above sea level, Hurricane Ridge stands at the northern rim of Washington's Olympic Mountains. Fully exposed to the incessant winter storms that pound in from the Pacific, conditions on the ridge can be ferocious. In excess of 30 feet of snow annually blanket these mountains. Though "blanket" conveys a sense of soft comfort. Instead, the snows pummel, pelt, bury, scour, ram, and suffocate Hurricane Ridge! Life exists in seasonally extreme ebbs and flows.

We drove to the ridge from near Sequim, where we enjoyed a bed and breakfast built recently in the architectural style of our first president's Mount Vernon. We could see both the Strait of Juan de Fuca and the Olympics from our two-night home. We ascended through full forest and within a narrow elevational band of thick fog (clouds). Douglas fir towered above us and thickets of sword fern flourished in their shade. We continued upward, viewing the sea of clouds beneath us and anticipating our eventual emergence into high country. The forest began yielding to alpine meadow and stunted trees as we neared the visitor's center. Summiting a final rise, we absorbed the stunning vista into the heart of the Olympics. At just under 8,000 feet, Mt. Olympus and her surrounding peaks seemed within reach. Snowfields, glaciers, and magnificent beauty proved hypnotic.

Nearby, deep green meadows splashed with summer's explosion of wildflowers beckoned to us. We followed a trail to the ridge summit. Now far below us, the clouds stretched to the horizon. Coarse, lee-deposited drifts of residual snow still stood 20 feet deep. Ravens lectured us from treetops; others foraged in the grass, occasionally joining the conversation. Deer grazed within touch, accustomed to human presence; they feasted on the abundant growth, knowing at some level that now is the time to grow fat with summer's bounty. The old drifts certainly provide direct evidence of nature's wintertime fury. The stunted trees bear testament that life can be tough, even at this elevation 2,000 feet below Mt. Olympus. Branches flagged to the east, barren on the west-facing windward exposure. Each wore a skirt of layering greenery, where under the deep winter snow they escape the wind's blasting.

Three solitary bears tirelessly foraged in the alpine buffet; they, too, were seemingly indifferent to our intrusion, though a fair distance away. Summer is short; fat is the ticket for surviving what lies ahead. Autumn will soon signal withdrawal from the mountaintop for the deer, bear, and the all-knowing wise one: the raven. This place of bounty and feasting will transition to inhospitable. Flora will begin shutting down, dormancy protecting it from winter's ravages. The annual cycle is rapid, predictable, wild, and everlasting. The mountains themselves seem uncaring and unaffected; yet their role is seminal, for they generate the extreme conditions and yield to their agents over the long sweep of time. Ageless tectonic processes continue to lift the Olympics, measurable with today's precise instrumentation. The weather wears them: heavy rains and snowmelt erode, avalanches and mudslides carry debris ever downward, freezing and thawing shatter and break surface features, glaciers scour powerfully.

Our lives likewise are shaped by our surroundings and experiences, even as we shape and mold those we touch. We bend to the cycles of time and events. We retreat and advance as the seasons of life stimulate action and reaction. Like the mountains, we feel and are shaped by countervailing forces lifting and eroding our faith, our character, our service to the future. Unlike the mountains, we can plan our future to some extent, choose our course, and envision the future we seek. The mountains know not tomorrow; they are simply there. As children of God, we must be as committed to tomorrow even as we navigate today. Like the bear and deer, for us a lapse of nature-directed judgment can lead us to suffering and death, both literal and actual. We too must observe and respond properly to the cycles and rhythms that swirl about us.

The natural world corroborates biblical teaching and validates the truth. Nature both teaches and inspires. Even without the explicit and metaphorical lessons from our trip to Hurricane Ridge, the beauty and wonder were sufficient to renew and reward us. A mountain odyssey pays dividends that can't be earned in our relatively flat Ohio. Wherever we live, God provides natural treasure and inspiration. But for me the mountain yields are greater, enriching me for the moment and adding a seasonal layer of life-sustaining and fulfilling memory and emotion: the spiritual "fat" to survive the winters of life.

I now bring another several years of deep living to my rearview perspective of visiting Hurricane Ridge. I have fruitfully explored and probed the concepts of nature based leadership and nature-inspired learning and leading over and over again, especially these past two years. I am jubilant to see my own words from a 63-months distance, "Nature both teaches and inspires." In fact, I wonder how many decades ago my mind already accepted that same sentiment, albeit perhaps not so explicitly and succinctly. Today, I preach the gospel of nature-inspired learning and leading—accepting, embracing, and applying nature's wisdom to life and work.

I once owned a canoe, only infrequently launching it when we lived in central Pennsylvania. I stored it under our back deck, drawing great comfort in knowing it was there, ready to rack and escape to a stream or lake. I look at the Hurricane Ridge trip in a parallel fashion. I know it is there; I can close my eyes and see summer's tranquility, and at the same time imagine winter's ferocity. I can only "see" that pleasurable terror through the lens of mental visualization. Even that view is powerful and compelling. The summer's brief immersion, along with my knowledge of what winter actually brings, is sufficient. I know I will never experience winter on Hurricane Ridge. They shutter the building and stop plowing in late fall. Yet I can still experience its lessons and find inspiration in its beauty, awe, magic, wonder, and ferocity.

Nature both teaches and inspires. These essays encapsulate nature's wisdom, amplify her inspiration, and seek ways to employ the lessons to living, learning, serving, and leading.

Great Blue Heron

~ Finding nature's inspiration through those now gone who shaped us ~

I offer these reflections as subtext to what I have come to accept as a given. That nature expresses every lesson for living, learning, serving, and leading across time, geography, and biome. That belief lies at the heart of my passion-fueled desire to give life and vibrancy to the emerging spirit and practice of nature-inspired learning and leading.

Dad died February 13, 1995. I was still running then. I did a ten-mile loop the morning of his memorial service, departing as dawn began painting the eastern sky. Single digit readings on the thermometer encouraged a quick early pace to bring warmth to my extremities. I floated—calm in the crisp silence, heading down to the winding road along Evitts Creek.

Northbound, the road flanked the creek's west bank, some 100 feet above the mostly ice-covered stream. Three and a half miles into the loop, movement at an ice-free sharp turn with mild rapids caught my eye. Hitting the stopwatch, I paused, looking east below me, squinting into the sun nosing above the ridge.

A great blue heron stood, shrouded in mist rising from the exposed water. We locked eyes, the magnificent bird watching me as intently as I gazed at him (I automatically assigned male gender, not wondering why). My quiet run had focused on thoughts of Dad and our many adventures in nature fishing, camping, hiking, and observing. He loved herons, their still, patient, deliberate, yet stilt-legged, awkward movements. Their lightning strike to nail a next meal. Their regal flight when, in lifting, those ungainly legs become one with the sleek flight profile.

We maintained eye contact for perhaps a minute, and then the heron rose, effortlessly. He was not headed up or down the waterway, but rising in slow spirals, ever skyward. I lost him when his flight crossed the rising sun, tears blurring my vision. I stood a moment, continuing to search the sky, but to no avail. I hit the stopwatch and resumed the loop, wiping tears as I ran. Dad had just said goodbye.

Since that long-ago winter morning, Dad occasionally makes a symbolic appearance: near a farm pond or a beaver dam, or in flight. The tears return. Warm memories flood. Dad is with me. He always will be.

Thanks to him, I am a lifetime outdoor enthusiast. I am convinced that nature communicates every lesson for living, learning, serving, and leading indelibly, repeatedly, and powerfully. Not all of nature's messages are lessons. Some are symbols, from which we draw inspiration and comfort. I know that Dad lives in me. Heron reminds me, freshens the memories, and deepens my gratitude. I suppose there is a lesson embedded in the imagery: that we all owe much to those who shaped us. That we should never forget that we grow from seeds others have sowed and nurtured. That nothing shapes us more than love.

Dad said goodbye, yet he holds me tightly. I should have thanked him more often, more clearly. He knows, I am sure. He occasionally stops by to tip his wings, grab a fish, or wade through the shallows.

Nature-inspired learning and leading: it's my passion; it's his spirit! Thank you, Dad.

Epilogue

I completed my book manuscript in March 2017. My mother passed away on April 17, 2017, a month after I submitted *Nature-Inspired Learning and Leading* to LifeRich Publishing. These closing thoughts are a fitting tribute to a person who helped shape me in so many ways, including sowing the seeds for my life dedicated to nature.

I gave Mom's eulogy on a spectacular Sunday along Patterson Creek in northern West Virginia. I cannot improve upon the message I presented to our gathered family and friends. I struggled, choked with emotion … finding the words far easier to have written than to speak. I realized that now there is no buffer between me and the next stage of my own Spirit's journey. A sobering reality, and yet a powerful motivation to make the most of what time remains. I feel both the inspiration of Mom's life and the humility of my own limitations. How can I possibly touch as many, and live so well in service to others?

Eulogy for Mom
April 30, 2017

Mom touched lives—mine … yours … and so many more. She lived for others—giving love, support, and care. She dedicated her life to family and friends—selfless beyond compare. I can speak only of the difference she made in my life … yet I know, she shaped you in ways just as powerful … just as lasting. I hope my tribute expresses feelings similar to your own sense of gratitude, appreciation, and reverence … for Helen Ruth Jones.

Mom passed peacefully—as she slept— in the pre-dawn of April 17, Easter Monday. Mom and I had said our goodbyes, mine moist with tears, just two weeks earlier. The last day of our visit, I handed her the words I had written the night before.

In that message, I reminded her that after she heard my eulogies for Dad ... and for Judy's mom, she asked me to write hers—not upon her death, but then. Right then! She wanted to read it in advance, rather than have me reserve it for this eventual memorial service. I refused. What if I wrote it and something happened to her? I didn't want to feel responsible for Mom's premature passing!

As it does, time marched on. As I wrote these words, Mom was in a nursing/rehabilitation center at age 92. Tired (more like weak and exhausted), hurting, and ill ... yet spiritually in comfort ... and at peace.

She said emphatically that she was ready (even eager) for release— release to her ultimate Home. She mentioned awaiting the chariot, "coming for to carry me home." I felt compelled that evening, before our next-day departure, to write what she had requested more than two decades earlier. Not yet a eulogy, but certainly the makings of one.

During our visit, Mom had asked me, "How did you become so interested in nature?" Someone entered her room before I could answer. I included my response in what I gave her.

I told her:

> You and Dad spoon-fed nature-enthusiasm to me. No, it was more like you pumped nature into me—a direct injection.
>
> You began by introducing me, through Grandma Jacobs, to flowering plants—annuals like petunias, marigolds, snapdragons, four-o'clocks, cleome, and other old favorites. We collected seeds, sowed them late winter indoors, nurtured the plantlets, and transplanted them outside. We watched the magic of germination, growth, and eventual flowering. We

continued through the cycle to seed collection, and preparation for yet another growing season.

You and Dad treated us to Sunday drives in the country, picnics, camping, immersing us in nature. Your efforts may not have consciously aimed to sculpt a naturalist—but still, you sowed the seeds. Metaphorically, you provided fertile soil, bright sunlight, room to grow, encouragement. Outdoor pursuits defined my early years ... and all the years since.

Nature courses through my veins—and it will until my own final heartbeat. You and Dad are responsible, whether your motives were intentional, or not. Your love and your nurturing (and yes ... your *naturing*) have made all the difference.

Nature is a thread that weaves through the fabric of my life. Nature is core to my heart, my mind, my body, my soul, and my spirit. You and Dad spun my life's nature thread from the fibers of nourishing outdoor experiences—rich with flowers, trees, forests, creeks, ponds, hills, mountains ... and love.

I spoke of the great blue heron in Dad's eulogy. When I see a great blue, I view it as Dad paying a visit, saying hello, keeping in touch.

I asked, "Mom, what's your favorite bird and why?"

She replied, without hesitation, almost as though she had anticipated the question, "Either the robin or the goldfinch. The robin because of his royal bearing and proud red breast." I could see Mom's mind at work—the robin's purposeful wanderings across the lawn, ear cocked for worm noise, always ready to pounce ... and extract a juicy meal. "The goldfinch, in part because of his bright color, but mostly due to his intensity." I imagined Mom's deep admiration of its rapid flittering hither and yon ... with deliberate purpose—and with seeming passion for its mission.

The great blue heron will always symbolize Dad ... from that day forward, Mom's symbol will be both the robin and the goldfinch—and she will live in my heart—long beyond her years, and through me to our kids ... and theirs ... and hence.

The written message I gave her continued:

> Robert Louis Stevenson spoke to the magic of touching the future: He said, "Don't judge each day by the harvest you reap, but by the seeds that you plant." To Mom I offered the following words of tribute:
>
> You and Dad sowed seeds that sprouted ... and now flourish as my internal tree of life—a tree that yields enriched living, learning, wisdom, truth, and love.
>
> I say now, to you and Dad, thank you for giving me *life*; for motivating me to *look*; for encouraging me to *see*; for enabling me to *understand*; for helping me to truly *appreciate* nature's power, wisdom, and inspiration.
>
> The great blue heron has now flown free for 22 years, since Dad's passing in 1995. My dearest mother, may the robin and goldfinch likewise feel flight's freedom ... and reach glorious heights. Please take my deep love and lasting appreciation with you—to what lies ahead in your Spirit's journey. May you, like Dad, "slip the surly bonds of Earth, and dance the skies on laughter-silvered wings ... put out your hand, and touch the face of God."

Mom read the words in my presence. She seemed pleased, and even a bit more at peace.

Blessedly, Mom's chariot arrived for her on schedule.

The morning after Mom passed, Judy and I watched two robins forage in our perennial beds—the first time that we've seen more than one at a time there. Twenty minutes later, as a shower approached from the southwest, our resident great blue heron flew from east to west just fifty feet above our shoreline, seeming close enough to touch. We saw him glance our way. Shortly after, the rain poured ... nourishing all that is alive and flourishing in this springtime of renewal.

I feel a great sense of relief, deep peace, and soothing calm. Mom and Dad signaled that morning that all is well. Joy fills my heart ... my soul, my spirit.

I know with absolute certainty—Mom and Dad are Home. And they live on in our hearts.

We are the fruits of the seeds they sowed.

May we all be worthy.

Stephen B. Jones Bio

Now 44 years beyond his bachelor's degree in forestry, Steve is devoting his life to championing the cause of Nature-Inspired Learning and Leading. He founded the Nature Based Leadership Institute at Antioch University New England in 2015 while serving as that institution's president—his third university presidency and eighth university. He preceded his 32 years in higher education with a dozen years in the paper and allied-products manufacturing industry where, among other assignments, he conducted tree nutrition and forest fertilization research for four years and served another two years in the Corporate Office of Environmental Affairs. As Alabama region land manager from 1981-84, he oversaw operations on the company's five hundred square miles of forestland across thirty-two counties. Steve has a bachelor's degree in forestry and a doctorate in natural resources management (applied ecology). Steve and Judy (his wife since June

1972) reside in the Tennessee Valley region of northern Alabama. Steve's ultimate intent is to enhance lives and enterprise success, even as he sows the seeds for responsible Earth stewardship. He is the CEO of Great Blue Heron, LLC (stevejonesGBH.com).

Steve is currently serving as Interim President Fairmont State University in Fairmont, West Virginia, effective July 1, 2017 through December 2017. Fairmont State is his ninth university and fourth university presidency.

Steve's first book is *Nature Based Leadership: Lessons for Living, Learning, Serving, and Leading* (LifeRich Publishing, December 2016). Watch for his third book: *Harnessing Nature's Wisdom and Inspiration.*

Cary H. Gaunt Bio, Author of the Foreword

Dr. Cary Gaunt focuses her leadership, management, and academic lens on ways to cultivate resilient, sustainable, and flourishing people and places. For more than twenty years she led sustainability and watershed management initiatives around the country as a planner, policy analyst, and program manager for Science Applications International Corporation (SAIC).

These experiences changed her trajectory as she grappled with understanding the root causes of environmentally unsustainable behavior. Her doctoral research at Antioch University New England and postdoctoral work at Naropa University explored the human behavior dimensions of sustainability, especially the life journeys and formative experiences of sustainability role models and leaders.

Dr. Gaunt translated her doctoral degree and prior sustainability management experience into consulting, and teaching in higher education. She is currently the Director of Campus Sustainability at Keene State College where she provides strategic visioning, planning, policy and curriculum development, and other overarching sustainability services for the campus.

TEALarbor stories
The Ecology & Art of Listening

TEALarbor stories' mission is to compassionately support people
as they discover & convey through writing their deepest stories.

*…using nature-based and creative processes for guidance
through writing, nature, & life's difficult landscapes…*

Writing Services
Consultations, Mentorship, Editing, Proofreading, Copywriting

Story & Nature Guiding©
Nature experiences for healing and insight

Life Transition Support
Practices for thriving during significant change, grief, loss

Mediated Conversations
Environmental Disputes, Family Disputes, Conflict Coaching,
Facilitated Conversations

*…offering individual guidance, small and large group
workshops, presentations, retreats, trainings, courses…*

Contact

Founder: Jennifer J. Wilhoit, Ph.D.

Email: tealarborstories@gmail.com

Website: www.tealarborstories.com

Blog: tealarborstories.blogspot.com

LinkedIn: www.linkedin.com/in/jenniferjwilhoit

Facebook: www.facebook.com/tealarborstories/

Twitter: twitter.com/TEALarbor

Great Blue Heron, LLC

Great Blue Heron (GBH), created, owned, and led by the author, serves and improves business, industry, organizations, and other enterprises via targeted consulting, speaking, and writing. GBH opens eyes to full appreciation of the limitless power of nature. GBH will show you, step-by-step, how to harness nature's wisdom and power, and apply it to your enterprise. We'll steer you toward channeling inspiration and humility, employing high purpose, and forging an intimate connection to nature applicable to your life and business endeavors.

Great Blue Heron understands that every lesson for living, learning, serving, and leading is either written indelibly *in*, or is compellingly inspired *by* nature. My ultimate intent is to enhance life and improve venture success, even as we together (you and GBH) sow the seeds for responsible Earth stewardship.

GBH strives to assist clients to:

- LOOK more closely
- SEE more completely
- FEEL deeply
- ACT with conviction and purpose

Great Blue Heron, LLC is purpose-driven, passion-fueled, and dedicated to changing lives, businesses, and organizations. I am president and CEO. A nature-enthusiast and grateful Earth citizen, I am GBH's lead scholar, principal author, primary consultant, and designated speaker.

Contact:

Great Blue Heron, LLC
213 Legendwood Drive NW
Madison, AL 35757
Steve@SteveJonesGBH.com
stevejonesGBH.com

Previously published book from Stephen B. Jones

Nature Based Leadership inspires, illuminates, and entertains those who are willing to learn from nature. A collection of personal reflections from a natural resources scientist, university president, philosopher, leadership scholar, nature enthusiast, and Earth citizen, this book evokes deep emotions and stimulates the reader to think deeply about our relationship with this planet we call home. The author walks a fine line between prose and lyricism. Some of these essays instruct of nature's pleasurable terror via the author's experience. Others do so through his tales of the power of nature's beauty, awe, wonder, and majesty. All of the essays draw indelible lessons from or inspired by nature. The lessons spur the reader to look, to see, to feel, and to act for the good of the individual, the enterprise, and our one Earth. These essays will leave you hungry for more of nature's wisdom and inspiration.

www.ingramcontent.com/pod-product-compliance
Lightning Source LLC
Chambersburg PA
CBHW020513290526
45786CB00002B/584